PROMOTING EMOTIONAL AND SOCIAL DEVELOPMENT IN SCHOOLS

A Practical Guide

Simon Blake with Julia Bird and Lynne Gerlach

P·C·P

Paul Chapman
Publishing

Paul Chapman Publishing
A SAGE Publications Company
1 Oliver's Yard
55 City Road
London EC1Y 1SP

SAGE Publications Inc
2455 Teller Road
Thousand Oaks, California 91320

SAGE Publications India Pvt Ltd
B 1/I 1 Mohan Cooperative Industrial Area
Mathura Road, New Delhi 110 044
India

SAGE Publications Asia-Pacific Pte Ltd
33 Pekin Street #02-01
Far East Square
Singapore 048763

Library of Congress Control Number: 2007924948

British Library Cataloguing in Publication Data

A catalogue record for this book is available from the
British Library

ISBN 978-1-4129-0730-9
ISBN 978-1-4129-0731-6 (pbk)

Typeset by C&M Digitals (P) Ltd, Chennai, India
Printed in Great Britain by the Cromwell Press, Trowbridge, Wiltshire
Printed on paper from sustainable resources

Dedication

This book is dedicated to all the children and young people who shared their ideas, experiences, joys and frustrations openly and honestly with frankness. They all had the ability to describe their often complex experiences with enviable directness and simplicity. In writing this book I hope we move some way closer to meeting your needs and supporting you to be brilliant and live the confident, healthy and fulfilling lives you imagine and desire.

And to Dylan, your Mum and Dad know this stuff backwards and use it daily to help you develop and grow. May your curiosity and confidence continue to flourish always. You are such a pleasure.

CONTENTS

Acknowledgements

Thank you to everyone who has provided ideas, support, material and case studies for this book. There are too many of you to name individually but I hope to have captured your experiences and wisdom honourably.

Thanks to colleagues and friends who regularly discussed ideas, concepts and issues with enthusiasm, telling stories and anecdotes that helped me understand. Thank you also for the support and time spent reading sections and drafts of this book, offering helpful insights, ideas and comments. Thanks, as always, to Tracey Anderson for excellent administrative support and making me laugh. Thank you to Joy Kumahor for administrative support in the final drafting stages.

And Sharon Munnings, here you go, your thank you! In this context what better to say than thank you for the hours of fun together, for being supportive, wise, insightful and sharp, and for teaching me about the importance of laughing as much and as often as you can.

The chapter for promoting young people's emotional health in Chapter 1 is reproduced with thanks to Cooperation and Working Together, a mental health initiative working across the North and Republic of Ireland.

Simon Blake

ABOUT THE AUTHORS

Simon Blake, lead author, was until September 2006 Assistant Director, Children's Development at the National Children's Bureau (NCB). He is a trainer, writer, advocate and campaigner for children's rights to high-quality Personal, Social and Health Education (PSHE), 'help' services and one-to-one advice and support. He led the NCB's Personal Social and Health Education programme and worked for both the Sex Education Forum and the Anti-Bullying Alliance. Whilst at the NCB Simon was a national assessor for the National Healthy Schools Programme; was seconded to the Department of Health to advise on children's policy including *Choosing Health*, the public health White Paper and *Healthy Schools*. He was co-editor of *Spotlight: Promoting Emotional and Social Development*, a regular magazine disseminated to schools and other settings across England. In 2005, Simon led the national consultation exercise on the feasibility of a National PSHE Subject Association funded by the Department for Education and Skills (DfES). In September 2006, Simon took up post as Chief Executive of Brook (www.brook.org.uk) the leading Voluntary sector provider of sexual health services, education and outreach for young people across the UK and Jersey.

Julia Bird and Lynne Gerlach of Sowelu Associates provided significant support, advice and guidance in the writing of this book. Much of their thinking and theoretical approach, and unique combination of experience as teachers, education consultants, Ofsted Inspectors and psychotherapists provided the foundations of the book. They advised on and contributed to all sections throughout the book and wrote the professional development chapter. Julia and Lynne have pioneered creative and positive approaches to supporting emotional and social development. They have developed new, exciting and accessible ways for practioners to turn theory and policy into practical interventions that support children. They are Directors of the first UK Master's Degree in Education: Emotional Literacy for Children (at the Institute for Arts in Therapy and Education). Lynne is also co-Director of the Integrative Arts Psychotherapy training and an assessor of Child Psychotheraphy trainees. Their work has inspired many schools to change the way they support vulnerable children and young people. They are part of a multi-professional team that developed the assessment and planning tool, ENABLE, an online resource (see Useful resources and organisations) and are co-authors of *Promoting Emotional Health and Well Being in Secure Units* (Bird and Gerlach, 2005a).

FOREWORD

I am so pleased that this book has been written; it is serious, based on research findings and is at the same time practical and accessible to teachers and those working in schools.

Many years ago I was excited about Daniel Goleman's first book on emotional intelligence. I knew it was important and, although it made sense to me in its application, I couldn't quite grasp the theory behind it.

I took the ideas and some of the practical suggestions to a group of young people I was working with in a Further Education college. And because I didn't quite understand the theory, I couldn't explain it very well and the young people were somewhat confused. So I suggested that we tried to develop some creative activities to define emotional intelligence. You can imagine my delight when they came up with wonderful collages; one depicted the *thinking heart* and the other the *feeling brain*. They did understand it after all and helped me to do so.

This book will help you to understand the theory and inspire you because when it is explained so well it's both exciting and obvious. It is also practical. I believe that it will become an essential handbook for busy people who want to apply all that new understanding of how the brain works and emotional development to make a real difference to children and young people's lives.

Gill Frances
Director, Children's Development
National Children's Bureau

Why this book matters

In schools the particular challenge (for the promotion of emotional and social development) is that there are so many children in a class and limited staff time. But how can children learn if their very basic needs are not being met, if they are hungry, scared or have had interruptions in their emotional and social development. It is for this reason that we must really help people understand the importance of robust and rigorous approaches to supporting emotional and social development. Only if we understand the way children and young people develop will we be able improve the emotional health and well-being, and therefore the learning, achievement, aspirations and health of the children and young people we work with. There is no alternative – I am completely convinced of that. (Bird, 2006)

Children and young people's emotional health is increasingly being recognised as important, not only in its own right, but because emotions play a significant role in learning. How we feel affects who we are and how we are, affects what we do, how we relate, how we get on, how we cope, the people we become and the world we create. Research in neuroscience has recently underlined the fact that emotional well-being is not a given; it is developed, and its healthy development can be influenced by the ways adults interact with children and young people. The quality of the relationship between them is key.

Frances Gilbert, a writer and teacher, writing in the *Times Educational Supplement* about emotional intelligence in August 2006, stated, the way we recognise other people's feelings, and our understanding and means of dealing with our own emotions are an essential part of growth. She goes on to discuss the important and central role of developing emotional intelligence amongst pupils in school as a vehicle for improving behaviour and promoting learning.

This book is based on the belief that promoting emotional health and well-being is important, and that children and young people are better able to learn in school if we respond positively and proactively to their emotional and social development needs. It is also based on a conviction that schools have a crucial role in developing children's and young people's emotional capacity – their resilience, their resourcefulness and their reflexivity – which in turn supports them to experience emotional well-being. This helps them manage their lives now, develop high aspirations and be well prepared for an exciting, stimulating and positive adult life.

At an international level, the World Health Organization has emphasised the importance of schools promoting mental health as part of their broad educational role in fostering healthy social and emotional development of pupils. They define child-friendly schools as one which:

encourages tolerance and equality between boys and girls and different ethnic, religious and social groups. It promotes active involvement and cooperation, avoids the use of physical punishment and does not tolerate bullying. It is also a supportive and nurturing environment providing education, which responds to the reality of the children's lives. Finally it helps to establish connections between school and family life, encourages creativity as well as academic abilities, and promotes the self-esteem and self-confidence of children. (World Health Organization, 2001: 1)

Children and young people themselves think that emotional health and well-being is crucial. When asked, they generally have a lot to say about the area. Many of those we have worked with have said that they would like more opportunities to consider what emotional health and well-being is, and that they have not really thought about it before. One young person described how just actually thinking about and talking with her peers about emotional health and well-being had helped her make the links between what she ate and how she felt, and the relationship between physical activity, sleep and emotional well-being.

The following definition of emotional health and well-being was developed by a group of young people from the North and Republic of Ireland who were involved in the *Getting It Together* project, a youth-led project addressing emotional health.

Emotional health is:

■ about how you feel inside;

■ about balancing your emotions and having control of them;

■ about self-esteem and confidence;

■ about being comfortable with who you are;

■ about coping with your feelings and building up resilience of your 'bounce-back ability'.

Others have defined emotional intelligence as having a *thinking heart* and a *feeling brain* thus emphasising a capacity to think whilst feeling.

Young people in the *Getting It Together* project developed the following charter setting out what they thought would be helpful for those working in schools and other services to do to promote emotional health and well-being. This is available as a poster that can be displayed in staffrooms and common rooms. It can also be used as a discussion starter in PSHE about your pupils' ideas and advice for services to promote emotional health and well-being (NCBs 2006).

Our charter for promoting young people's emotional health

Emotional health is:

■ about how you feel inside;

■ about balancing your emotions and having control of them;

■ about self-esteem and confidence;

■ about being comfortable with who you are;

(Continued)

(Continued)

■ about coping with your feelings and building up resilience and your 'bounce-backability'.

It is important to promote young people's emotional health, because it is about how we feel, and how we feel affects what we do, how we get on, how we cope and the people we will become.

Here are some things you can do to promote young people's emotional health:

■ Organise activities to build trust between professionals and young people, and among young people and their friends.

■ Display posters and run workshops in schools and community settings on emotional health and young people.

■ Undertake outreach activities and take services to young people.

■ Advertise helplines, use emails to advise young people about local services and one-to-one advice and support.

■ Use national campaigns such as Mental Health Day to raise awareness of emotional health.

■ Make links to other aspects of health such as healthy eating, stress reduction and physical activity.

■ Use residentials, fun days and other strategies to promote friendships and team building and provide new experiences.

We want adults who:

■ Understand that the way they treat us in everyday life affects our confidence, our self-esteem and our emotional health. We don't want to be treated like children, but don't expect us to be adults either.

■ Communicate well with us and listen to what we think and how we feel.

■ Encourage us to broaden our horizons and try new things.

■ Ask us what we want and make sure we are involved in decisions that affect us – and don't just ask, action it and involve us in the solutions to problems.

■ Understand and remember what it felt like to be young and recognise that we are young and we need to learn our own lessons and make our own mistakes.

■ Don't put us under too much pressure.

To be confident in services we have to be sure that services are confidential. One of the biggest things that stops young people accessing services is our fear that people will gossip about us getting help.

Reproduced with thanks to Cooperation and Working Together – A mental health initiative working across the North and Republic of Ireland.

This book is based on research, and the practical experience of a wide range of professionals working in and with schools, who have shared their ideas, successes and challenges with National Children's Bureau and Sowelu Associates over the last decade within the context of development projects and training across the UK, Ireland and beyond.

The book is divided into three main parts. The first provides an overview of the theory and evidence about emotional health, children and young people. It provides an important framework for everyone in schools trying to promote emotional well-being, positive behaviour, achievement and health. It brings together different strands of thinking to help you understand the range of actions and interventions schools can develop as both preventative and reactive strategies.

It also provides a brief overview of the policy context in England – even though this book is written for an international audience, this is purposely included as a case study, because there have been some important developments in children's policy in England in recent years that will be of benefit to others.

Chapters 3–8 focus on translating theory to practice. These chapters set out the range of issues relating to policy development, establishing policy and partnerships and offer a range of practical tried and tested ideas for promoting emotional and social development in schools. These are illustrated with a range of quotes from children and young people as well as case studies to motivate, inspire you and remind you that this is not an optional extra, or a desirable add on, but absolutely core to enabling children and young people, to grow, play and learn with confidence and enthusiasm.

Chapter 9 provides practical guidance and some introductory activities to support a whole school focus on emotional and social development. These can be used in an in-service training session (INSET), a series of staff meetings or a combination of the two.

Effective 'joining up'

Children and young people need adults in education, health and care who are willing to hold them, to hold boundaries, to understand them, to listen to them and to help them work out what they need. It is not going to work to go in with a bit more drug education or a bit more Citizenship education to meet specific policy objectives. Sure these are important, but it is much more complicated than that. We need to identify where there have been interruptions in children's emotional and social development and work out what emotional development steps need to be revisited and relearned so they can move forward. It is only through true relationship with children and young people that we can do this without alienating or blaming them for the symptoms of these interruptions; symptoms that dominate the media and public policy debates – antisocial behaviour, teenage pregnancy, substance misuse etc. (Bird, 2006)

This emphasises the need to think about the holistic and joined-up nature of children's lives and the importance of responding to their needs in an equally joined-up and holistic way. It highlights how the promotion of emotional health and well-being lies at the centre of our efforts to improve outcomes for children and young people. Children and young people tell us time and again that education and support is often offered in relation to specific issues such as sex or alcohol and other drugs and, as a result, can feel irrelevant or dislocated from their experience (Blake, 2005).

Antidote (a campaign for emotional literacy) believes that emotional literacy has a vital part to play in tackling the multiple challenges facing our communities, by enabling people to:

- Find ways of feeling connected to each other, and of using their relationships to process the emotions that might otherwise cause them to lash out in rage or to withdraw in despair

- Deal with the emotions that can render them unable to take in new information, and to access emotional states such as curiosity, resilience and joy that lead to a richer experience of learning

- Engage in activities that promote both physical and emotional well-being, and to broaden the range of issues they can talk about with each other in ways that make it less likely they will abuse drugs and alcohol, bully their peers or engage in other forms of self-destructive activity

Below are some real-life examples where an approach based on the ostensible issues is unlikely to be successful unless coupled with support or learning in relation to emotions and emotional literacy.

Example 1– Bullying

Children who are hurt and abused will often hurt and bully other children. An effective response is one where the immediate response to the bullying behaviours ensures that those bullied are safe and feel safe, that there is a visible commitment to stopping the bullying and that the child or young person doing the bullying takes responsibility for their behaviour and makes amends.

This is coupled with longer-term support to identify and address any deep-rooted hurt and emotional distress that contributes to the child needing to behave in harmful and antisocial ways. For example, have they experienced interruptions in their emotional and social development, which mean they need help to develop empathy or skills for working with others?

Example 2

Young people in public care are significantly overrepresented as teenage parents (Corlyon and McGuire, 1999). This has been associated with a desire for inclusion, to achieve some social status, to assert a sense of independence, freedom and agency, and to be able to provide the love and stability for their baby that they themselves have not experienced. Providing good sex and relationships education and excellent sexual health services is obviously important. Yet efforts to reduce the levels of teenage pregnancy amongst this group requires additional approaches that respond to their emotional and social development needs, and offers age appropriate experiences that respond to their individual concerns and issues. All of Brook's services include counselling and emotional support as part of clinical service provision. This is also supported by outreach to support vulnerable groups. Further information is available on www.brook.org.uk.

Example 3

Children and young people experiencing loss or grief through parental divorce, separation or bereavement may misbehave in class and interrupt others or withdraw and stop trying at their schoolwork. In many cases these types of behaviours are punished or controlled through sanctions. This approach alone can simply serve to reinforce or heighten their emotional state and steps need to be taken to respond to the underlying emotional needs through a range of interventions such as peer support or one-to-one counselling rather than controlling the seen behaviours.

Case study: Adopting a holistic approach – working with young black people

The Black Health Agency works with young people on issues of sexual and emotional health. Through a peer-based project they work in and with schools in the Greater Manchester area. Although originally funded to focus on sexual health, they very quickly learnt from those they worked with that if they were going to have any impact on the quality of relationships and public health targets such as teenage pregnancy, they would need to address a wider range of 'emotional' issues or core issues and experiences that affected their sense of confidence and self-esteem.

The issues that young people identified as impacting on their relationships included:

- Experiences of racism and discrimination
- Experiences of poor housing and poverty
- Experiences of schooling
- Their families' and communities' attitude to schooling
- Their own hopes, beliefs and dreams for the future

The project, Young Peerspectives, now takes a broader and much more holistic approach to addressing and promoting self-confidence and self-esteem as core to the development of strong emotional health and well-being.

For further information visit www.blackhealthagency.org.uk.

Looking beneath the surface: understanding what behaviours tell us

Children and young people's behaviour is a barometer for their emotional health and well-being. It tells us about the ways in which they have learned to manage emotional discomfort and stress. Children need help from the adults around them to learn how to recognise, regulate, communicate and express their emotions. Adults are role models; the ways in which they act and react to children show children how to manage and how to be. At best, the adults who are working with children and young people need to be able to recognise, manage and contain their own emotional states so that they can show, in the detail of their relationships with the young people, just what emotional literacy looks like.

Emotional states are accompanied by bodily sensations, which is why we commonly call them 'feelings' – we literally feel differently when we experience being happy or sad or angry or scared for example. Some bodily states are undeniably powerful. If we are gripped by terror or rage, our instincts take over and some basic survival behaviours get triggered to deal with it – we run away, or we fight or we freeze. Most of the time when we are not experiencing extreme emotional states we can actually use our feelings to help us to choose how to be and what to do.

For example, Jake, 13 years old, sees a really exciting experiment in a physics lesson and he is intrigued. His curiosity is aroused and he feels excited and keen to know more. He feels aroused, connected, interested. He decides to concentrate harder and he focuses his energy and attention on what to do next to give him more of those good feelings.

There are many children who are unable to think about or explain what they are feeling. This makes it hard to make choices about what to do. A child flooded with strong emotion who has not learned how to contain and regulate it, is much more likely to discharge the feeling into an 'acting out' behaviour. If the feeling is overwhelming, the child is less likely to be able to think about it, or to be able to think at all and they will not be able to make a choice about their behaviour. Helping children to recognise and regulate their emotional states is a key precursor to children being able to take responsibility for their behaviours.

Children learn about emotions and how to handle them through their experience of being in relationship with adults. If Mummy gets distressed and upset when the child is sad, the child soon learns to cover up sadness. If Daddy gets depressed when the child asks for help, the child learns to get help elsewhere – or not ask for it. If the teacher gets angry when the child does not understand or makes a mistake, the child learns to avoid making mistakes or covers up when they do not get it – when that is not possible they might choose to limit the risks they take and so stop trying things out. If the carer takes strong feelings in her or his stride, accepts they happen and communicates that they are survivable, the child feels contained and safe, and the world feels manageable.

All children need help from caring adults to learn how to manage their feelings. By the time children come into nursery or infant school, they will already have learned a lot about feelings: which are acceptable, which not; how to deal with them in ways that are like their carers, and that their carers like; how to avoid situations that are emotionally too uncomfortable; what helps; what to do in emergencies. For some children, everyday situations can feel like emergencies most of the time – they feel on 'red alert' and ready to respond with basic survival strategies of fight or flight at the slightest hint of threat or trouble.

A 9 year-old child in a pupil referral unit (PRU) who lived with his mother who had serious substance misuse habits would become very angry when he was asked to do something or told what to do. This had been identified as a behavioural issue until he revealed that he was witnessing severe domestic violence at home on a daily basis. Through enquiry and active listening to his story and multidisciplinary action, support was provided to help him learn to manage his feelings in school. His mother was also offered family support to enable change in the home circumstances.

Other children adopt different coping strategies and appear to take everything in their stride. Real-life experiences, which would make many people quiver, are part of the everyday fabric of these children's lives. Often their pride and their courage means they compensate by being quiet, try to go unnoticed, work tremendously hard at school, or always make sure, within their physical and emotional means, that they participate as well as they possibly can at school. Batmanghelidjh (2006), for example, describes the story of a young woman let down and hurt by almost everyone in her life, who made sure she was always immaculately dressed for school. This was after all one area she could control.

Children offer us, through a range of behaviours, clues and signals about how they feel. Their behaviours indicate what they have learned so far about how to use and manage their feelings; these include both the difficult feelings such as anger, rage and jealousy and the positive arousal feelings such as pleasure, excitement and curiosity. Adults who understand about emotional development can assess how well the child is managing their emotional states by observing the child's behaviour. The range of feelings a child is comfortable to deal with and the ways in which they is have learned to deal with them are both important elements in their social development. Children can then be supported by caring adults to do the next needed piece of emotional learning, which will include (a) broadening the range of emotions they can recognise, regulate and communicate and (b) extending the range of thinking options, choices and behavioural strategies the child has to make good use of the emotions she or he experiences.

This has been recognised in the Primary and Secondary National Strategies for Education in England, both of which have a key focus area on promoting the developing of skills, which enable children, and young people to manage their emotions and ask for help. Information about the two programmes can be found on the www.bandapilot.org.uk and www.standards.dfes.gov.uk websites.

Similarly, *Choosing Health*, the public health White Paper published by Department of Health in 2005 identifies the relationship between emotional health and well-being and physical health outcomes such as teenage pregnancy, substance misuse and obesity. It is only through supporting children and young people's emotional and social development that we will make an impact in areas of public policy concern.

Child-focused policy: A case study of English policy

This section briefly summarises the English policy context for children. Although this book has been written for an international audience, the English policy context is an interesting case study as great strides have been made in developing a holistic approach to children's health, well-being and achievement. Similar developments are taking place across the UK and many other parts of the world, although the initiatives and strategies are called different names.

Following extensive consultation with children and their families, there are now five national outcomes enshrined in law that all professionals working with children and young people must work towards achieving:

- Being healthy
- Staying safe
- Enjoying and achieving
- Making a positive contribution
- Economic well-being

Schools are required to demonstrate how they are contributing to these through their Office for Standards in Education (Ofsted) Inspections (further information about the process is available from www.ofsted.gov.uk).

All children's policy in England is set to align with this agenda in the coming years and a major strategic programme of reorganisation and workforce development is being implemented at national, regional and local levels. Significantly, this includes a commitment to developing a common core-training programme, which means that all professionals working with children will be trained to understand the process of children's development.

This is a radical programme of change aiming to integrate all services for all children aged 0–19. The programme of change places schools at the centre of the development of child-focused services. It includes the joining up of services, the Extended Schools Programme, for further information visit www.teachernet.gov.uk, a greater focus on early intervention, support for parents and carers as well as access and referral to specialist services that are provided on the school site and in the community.

There are a number of strategies across education and health, which address different aspects of learning, achievement and health and well-being. These include the Primary and Secondary National Strategies, which focus on the promotion of emotional and social development. In primary schools this programme is called Social and Emotional Aspects of Learning and is being implemented in a significant number of schools across England. The materials are available to download at www.bandapilot.org.uk.

A package of secondary materials is currently being piloted in England. These materials focus on the development of Social, Emotional and Behavioural Skills. Further information about the materials can be found at www.standards.dfes.gov.uk.

Children's policy across different government departments is also working towards this holistic framework. For example, the Children and Young People's Public Health Programme, responsible for delivery of the children's section of Choosing Health is supporting the Young People's Development Programme which offers young people opportunities for personal development, challenge and risk (see providing opportunities for adventure and risk, page 81 for further information).

The national Blueprint Drugs Research Programme has funded the development of guidance on wider aspects of Personal, Social and Health Education, including the promotion of emotional health and well-being in recognition of the links between physical health and emotional health (De Silva and Blake, 2006). Personal, Social, Health Education and Citizenship provide a curriculum focus for the planned provision of opportunities for emotional and social development. Through PSHE and Citizenship children learn and develop the skills, confidence and abilities to understand themselves, their relationships with others, how to look after their physical and emotional health and their rights and responsibilities as citizens. Through Citizenship children and young people have opportunities for active participation in school and the community. These opportunities are central to children and young people's emotional and social development as they promote engagement, empathy, self-esteem, self-worth and confidence. In addition, they provide opportunities to develop relationships with others and understand the potential for their behaviour to have a positive impact on others.

The Teenage Pregnancy Strategy is supporting the development of integrated PSHE provision as opposed to a narrow focus on sex and relationships. The two separate Independent Advisory Groups on Teenage Pregnancy and Sexual Health and HIV that advise government have led an investigation and are calling for PSHE to be made statutory (TPIAG and SHIAG, 2005) alongside the further development of visible high-quality services for young people that address their sexual and emotional health.

The National Healthy Schools Programme is a major programme, jointly funded by the Department of Health and the Department for Education and Skills, aiming to improve health and well-being, improve educational attainment and reduce social and health inequalities. It is based on the premise that children need to be healthy to learn and that those children who learn and achieve well at school tend to lead healthier lives into and throughout adulthood.

The programme is a vehicle through which schools can identify their priorities, local issues and concerns, and through a structured process develop an action plan, including the expected outcomes and measurement. The promotion of emotional health and well-being is one of four key areas that schools need to address to achieve healthy school status.

The four areas are inextricably interlinked. They are emotional health and well-being, PSHE, diet and nutrition, and physical activity. The following criteria are used by schools as the 'standard' for emotional health and well-being against which to measure and evaluate themselves.

A healthy school

1 Identifies vulnerable individuals and groups and establishes appropriate strategies to support them and their families

2 Provides clear leadership to create and manage a positive environment which enhances emotional health and well-being in school – including the management of the behaviour and rewards policies

3 Has clear, planned curriculum opportunities for pupils to understand and explore feelings using appropriate learning and teaching styles

4 Has a confidential pastoral support system in place for pupils and staff to access advice – especially at times of bereavement and other major life changes – and this system actively works to combat stigma and discrimination

5 Has explicit values underpinning positive emotional health which are reflected in practice and work to combat stigma and discrimination

6 Has a clear policy on bullying, which is owned, understood and implemented by the whole school community

7 Provides appropriate professional training for those in a pastoral role

8 Provides opportunities for pupils to participate in school activities and responsibilities to build their confidence and self-esteem

9 Has a clear confidentiality policy

Personal Social and Health Education has a key role to play in achieving some of these standards. The Healthy Schools Programme also emphasises the importance of a whole-school approach, which includes effective leadership and management, pupil participation, involvement of parents, carers and the wider community, and the importance of meeting the needs of those who are marginalised and vulnerable.

Further information about the National Healthy Schools Programme is available from www.wiredforhealth.gov.uk.

It is important to note that despite this excellent policy development and intention, there is still a tendency for practice to be fragmented and uncoordinated. The immediate challenge is to maximise the opportunities available to ensure the best support for children, young people and their families. Through Every Child Matters and the Extended Schools Programme, schools lie at the heart of this aspiration of joining up and providing child centre services.

'Good enough' emotional health and well-being

The following sets out the qualities, experiences and perceptions that someone with 'good enough' emotional health and well-being should have and will be working towards:

- A secure sense of who they are (this will clearly change over time and as they grow and develop)

- A sense of being able to be themselves which is accompanied by aliveness, vitality and energy

- A sense of belonging and connection to a few significant people

- A sense of self worth that sustains them in the face of setbacks

- A belief in their own ability to influence things and make changes

- An ability to identify, ask for and move towards the things they need

- An ability to recognise, care about and take responsibility for the impact of their behaviour on others

- A willingness and ability to do things with others and or alone

- A capacity to tolerate uncertainty and respond creatively and with integrity to the challenges life brings

- A capacity to respect the need for appropriate boundaries for self and others

- A way of making sense of their experience to sustain them through life's challenges. (Bird and Gerlach, 2005)

Children and young people need the opportunities, experiences and relationships to enable them to build this sense of emotional health and well-being throughout their school life.

CHAPTER 2

An overview of the evidence from research and practice

This chapter summarises the evidence from research and practice. It offers:

■ Some facts about children, young people and emotional and mental health and well-being
■ A summary of why emotional health and well-being is important for learning
■ Information and examples about the importance of caring relationships between adults in school and children and young people
■ The learning from the growing stable of brain research and the process of emotional and social development
■ Information about building emotional resilience

Some facts about children, young people and emotional and mental health

The Schools Health Education Unit examined trends between 1983 and 2003 in young people's emotional health and well-being as reported through their young people and health survey they found that young people:

■ Are increasingly more likely to worry 'quite a lot/a lot' about school and career problems

■ Are now more likely to share school-based problems with mum and dad, or a teacher and friend than those two decades ago

■ Are less likely to worry about 'the way they look', although it is important to note that for around 50 per cent of young women this was still the main problem (SHEU, 2004).

A survey found that 60 per cent of young people said that they needed to be taught how to cope with stress – more than they wanted help on drugs, money or sex. More than one in five of the young people said that they felt highly stressed 'most of the time'. By far the biggest cause of stress for this group was schoolwork and examinations, with over 70 per cent identifying these factors as causing stress (Stockdale and Katz 2002).

ChildLine, the UK's helpline for children and young people, regularly provide an analysis of calls to the helpline focusing on different issues. In their recent publications on calls about emotional and mental well-being (Easton and Carpentieri, 2004); eating disorders (McConville, 2003) and volatile substance abuse (Blake and Navidi, 2005) they identify how difficult situations and circumstances lead to poor emotional health and well-being, which underlies these self-damaging behaviours. For example:

■ Talking about sexual abuse, one young woman told ChildLine that she felt she had no right to expect anyone's care and attention and that anyone who knew 'what had happened' would not want to see or touch her, let alone care for or love her. Convinced that she was both undeserving and to blame, she had not been able to speak to anyone about her past and had become increasingly depressed over the course of her youth (Easton and Carpentieri, 2004: 30)

■ I've had my head down the toilet every morning, afternoon and evening. Feel complete and utter shite, but wore my smile, so everyone left me alone. My Gran commented on how happy I am all the time, but I'm really not … (McConville, 2003: 11)

■ Dad doesn't trust me and mum always expects me to keep the house tidy. I don't get on with either of them. I started sniffing aerosols at the end of last year. Since then I moved on to glue. I cut myself and I've taken paracetemol to try to commit suicide. I hate school and I don't care … (Blake and Navidi, 2005: 14)

The largest ever study into self-harm has shown that more than one in 10 teenage girls harms themselves each year. The authors (Hawton et al. 2006) concluded that the problem is far more widespread than was thought. They identified its links to bullying at school, physical and sexual abuse and being worried about being gay. The authors said that self-harming is so common that it is 'the most pressing health issue for teenagers'.

It is important to recognise that some of these behaviours are important ways in which young people regain a feeling of power and control in the face of feeling powerless or out of control in other aspects of their lives. As one young person (in McConville, 2003: 13) said, 'I live on air, how powerful is that?'.

Bullying is one of children and young people's main concerns. In 2004/05, ChildLine counselled 32,688 children about bullying. Bullying accounted for 25 per cent of the calls to ChildLine and was the most common reason children call the helpline. The Children's Commissioner has said that bullying is the biggest concern that children and young people contact him about (Blake and Crow, 2005). Bullying can destroy children and young people's enjoyment of school, family and social life, as well as their capacity to learn in the long term as well as immediately. One study found that primary school children who were bullied were more likely to report disturbed sleep, bed-wetting, feeling sad, headaches and stomach aches. The risk of these symptoms increased with the frequency of the bullying (Williams et al., 1996). Children and young people who are bullied often truant from school. They can be more anxious and insecure than those who are not bullied, and suffer from low self-esteem and see themselves as failures. In the longer term, bullying can lead to anxiety, lack of confidence, self-harm and depression. In the most serious cases children and young people attempt suicide, with a small number killing themselves.

The prejudice and discrimination experienced by young people as a result of their sexual orientation, home experiences, ethnicity or disability often has an impact on their self-esteem and confidence. For example:

- Some young people may feel unaccepted by their community in the school or outside. Many experience being humiliated, ostracised or treated badly because of their sexuality, but any feature that is different from the norm may be picked on to justify bullying behaviour including size, accent, personal habits, and so on

- Some young people who have themselves experienced being badly treated or even abused, feel so badly about themselves they resort to self-harm. Blake (2003: 47) quotes a young gay man describing watching his friend hurt himself, 'For a long time I just used to have to stand by while he did this to himself. I knew that he was really screwed up because he was gay'

- Research in mainly white schools in 2001/02 found that 25 per cent of pupils from minority ethnic backgrounds had experienced racist name-calling within the last week. A third reported hurtful name-calling and verbal abuse either at school or during the school journey, and for more than 16 per cent this was persistent (DfES, 2002)

- Mencap reported in 2000 that nearly 90 per cent of people with a learning disability experience bullying, with over 66 per cent of them experiencing it on a regular basis

- Mason and Palmer (1996) in their report on hate crimes against lesbians and gay men reported 50 per cent of violent attacks involved fellow students and 40 per cent of the attacks actually took place at school. Worryingly, some of the prejudice they experience: comes from adults as well as peers. One young woman described her experience: 'some staff already knew (I was gay) but my form teacher wanted to know the full story herself. I was being beaten up by some girls in my class because I was gay. In the end I told my form teacher … her once caring attitude towards me changed … at first she told me, I wasn't, you know, gay … I've been told by her I'm going to hell and that I'm concerned with things that shouldn't be thought by anyone, let alone girls of my age' (p. 60)

Horton (2005) provides an overview of some key statistics relating to children, young people and mental health:

- 11 per cent of boys and 8 per cent of girls have a mental disorder[1]

- 15 per cent of pre-school children have mild mental health problems and 7 per cent have a severe mental health problem

- Approximately 10 per cent of children and young people have mental health problems that are severe enough to require professional help

- McConville (1999) identified the growing concern about mental health of young men, which is reflected in the almost doubling of the suicide rate in the 1990s with suicide being the second most common cause of death among young men

---

[1] Mental disorders are a clinically recognisable set of symptoms or behaviour associated with considerable distress and substantial interference with personal functions.

■ Children are less likely to develop mental health problems if they have good communication skills, a sense of humour, the capacity to reflect, at least one good parent-child relationship. Good housing, a range of positive sporting and leisure activities (Mental Health Foundation, 2001)

The National Healthy Schools Programme in England has identified the following factors as the things that have the biggest positive impact on the emotional well-being of children and young people:

■ Having people to talk to

■ Personal achievement

■ Being praised

■ Generally feeling positive about oneself

And the key things that make them feel stressed are:

■ Conflict

■ Confrontation with authority

■ Restriction of autonomy

■ Exclusion by their peers (Ahmad et al., 2003)

The National Health and Lifestyle Surveys in Ireland (2002), as part of their survey on general health, asked how happy children felt about their lives at present. Overall 43 per cent reported that they are very happy and a further 45 per cent that they are quite happy with their lives. The remaining 11 per cent report that they are not very or not at all happy.

Evidence shows that many children try to manage difficult emotions and get unmet needs met through destructive behaviours. Whilst it would be untrue to say that risk-taking only occurs when people do not have a positive sense of self, it is well documented that children and young people with a poor sense of self, low self-esteem and poor emotional health and well-being are much more likely to demonstrate behaviours which mean they experience lower academic achievement and poorer health outcomes. For example, many children and young people with poor emotional health and well-being will enter into sexual relationships to try and get their emotional needs met. This often renders them more vulnerable as it is unlikely their emotional needs will be met within these relationships.

Violence and abuse is commonplace in the lives of many children and young people and is known to have an impact on the health and well-being of children and young people. Many children calling ChildLine describe the violence they are experiencing and the impact on their lives.

■ I'm so upset. My parents keep hitting me. I'm covered in bruises. Mum slaps me for not doing the dishes, or going to bed early. My father punches me and makes me upset' (Blake and Navidi, 2005: 25)

'Behind closed doors: the impact of domestic violence on children' (Unicer, 2005) showed that in the UK almost a million children experience domestic violence. The report says that as many as one in 14 children in the UK may receive poor examination results as a result of domestic violence at home and that children may experience a range of effects, including low self-esteem, aggression and adjustment problems.

In addition the evidence shows the scale of violence and abuse in the UK:

■ In 2004 there were 32,700 children on the child protection register

■ 20 per cent of 18–24-year-olds report some serious maltreatment by parents during their childhood

■ 16 per cent of children have suffered sexual abuse

■ Over a third report an absence of care

■ 75 per cent tell no one about their experiences

■ The economic cost of child abuse is estimated at £1 billion per year (McVeigh et al., 2005)

Data extracted from the Young Life and Times Survey in Northern Ireland (Cairns and Lloyd, 2005) summarised the levels of psychological distress[2] experienced by 16-year-olds. They concluded:

■ 30 per cent of young women and 16 per cent of young men fell into the psychologically distressed category

■ School work and examinations was the most cited cause of stress

■ Young men identified financial problems followed by family problems as the next biggest causes of stress

■ Young women identified family problems followed by being under pressure as their next biggest causes of stress

■ 13 per cent of young people reported being bullied at school. (This is lower than statistics in England.) Where people reported being bullied there was a significant relationship between this and levels of psychological distress

Children with emotional disorders (separation anxiety, social phobia, specific phobia, generalised anxiety, depression) are more likely to have been excluded from school than other children (12 per cent compared with 4 per cent), more likely to be behind in their overall intellectual development (44 per cent compared with 24 per cent), and more likely to truant (16 per cent compared to 3 per cent) (Green et al., 2005).

Body image and concerns about the way young people look is traditionally associated with girls and young women. McConville (1998: 40–1) quotes 65 per cent of young women aged 15 and 16 would like to change a part of their body compared with 39 per cent of young men. Evidence from research and practice demonstrates that both boys and girls are concerned about how they look (Wren, 2006).

Why is emotional health and well-being important for learning and achievement?

Goleman (1996) argues that emotion is central to the development of morality and learning. He argues that we need to encourage capacities such as persistence, zeal and the ability to motivate oneself.

---

[2] They describe psychological distress based on the 12-item General Health Questionnaire (O'Reilly and Stevenson, 2003) focusing on issues such as sleep loss due to worry, anxiety, loss of confidence and concentration and general happiness.

This section summarises brain research, the process of brain development and how this impacts on children's ability to think and learn.

Babies first develop their sense of themselves in relation to key adults in their lives. Babies' brains develop significantly over the first two years of life. The care that they receive directly influences the development of neural pathways in the brain. The baby literally learns how to cope with stress through her or his experience in relationship to the primary carers. The brain then gets wired to deal with stress and strong emotions in particular ways – which in turn determines the behaviours she or he uses to manage these emotions.

Our early experiences of depending on a significant other colour and inform the ways we think about ourselves in relation to the world. The quality of this attachment is central to children's emotional health and well-being (Bowlby, 1969). So when babies and children experience generally positive relationships, which are responsive, supportive, containing, caring and warm, their brain becomes 'hard-wired' to respond to others in a similar way. Loving interactions where babies are valued and their distress is soothed by a primary care-giver help shape the brain for resilience to stress. Chemical and hormonal reactions are stimulated which, in turn, develop neuronal pathways resulting in the ability to be calm and to think.

A child will remember and learn from these early experiences and come to make sense of their world based on this. Where these experiences are 'good enough' they will feel safe and develop trust in adults. The trust is essential to emotional health and well-being and provides the building blocks through which others (for example their peers) can contribute to a positive sense of self and their identity as they grow.

The opposite of this is also true. If a baby's or child's' early experience of relationships are uncaring, distant, inconsistent, neglectful, frightening or abusive their brain becomes 'hard-wired' to respond to others as if everyone will relate in these ways. The child adopts defensive behaviours to protect themselves from these imagined, anticipated experiences. When the baby or child consistently experiences these unpredictable, frightening, neglectful or abusive reactions, they learn to expect relationships that are filled with uncertainty, fear, anger, distance and distress. As a result the world feels unsafe and as neuronal pathways are established, instinctive responses of fight, flight and freeze become hard-wired into the brain. These instinctive responses block access to thinking and, of course, learning.

As a child grows, those with poor early experiences are more likely to experience anxiety, fear and hopelessness, as well as rage and hatred as they experience these feelings. If they do so without access to their thinking skills, behaviours can develop which are likely to be considered disruptive in school and the family. Seen as the cause rather than the symptom, these behaviours often generate a negative response, which does not help and can perpetuate the feelings including rage. What children and young people really need in this situation is an experience of being soothed and calmed down by someone with whom they have a strong relationship so they can learn new behaviours and new skills for managing their feeling.

The brain development research is, thankfully, showing us that planned work and strong positively caring and consistent relationships with adults can undo much of the early 'negative hardwiring'. To enable this to happen we need to pay close attention to the behaviours that children and young people are demonstrating so we are able to identify the types of interruptions in their emotional and social development and provide suitable, age-appropriate experiences that enable this type of reparation.

Emotional Needs, Achievement, Behaviour and Learning (ENABLE) is a computer package, which assesses and identifies emotional needs from the behaviours that children are displaying. It suggests differentiated practical strategies for adults to use in one-to-one, small-group or classroom situations to address unmet emotional needs and allow for the next and needed learning to happen. It relies on positive human interaction to develop reparative relationships in which children can learn to manage their feelings differently so that they have more choice about how to behave. The computer-generated action plans support those who work in school (and other care or learning situations) to develop approaches and activities that will contribute to the emotional and social development the children need to learn and succeed.

The case study below provides an overview of how ENABLE has been used in a primary school.

Case study: Using ENABLE in South Brent Primary School, Devon.

South Brent Primary School has been working on the 'ENABLE project' since 2004. ENABLE is a computer software programme, which helps workers understand children's emotional and social development needs by reviewing their behaviours. These are considered in the context of their general personal, family and school history.

Based on this assessment a range of one-to-one and small-group activities are chosen to address the child's particular needs. Other suggestions about helpful classroom, learning environment and teaching and curriculum approaches are developed through this review.

The ENABLE project in the school combined the use of the software with a commitment to developing an 'ENABLE' approach and philosophy across all staff towards addressing emotional health and well-being. The project therefore included a number of components, which were:

- Demonstration of the ENABLE software for staff and conducting model assessment sessions, both with and without staff
- Training of the School Leadership Team, teachers and learning support staff in the approach and philosophy of ENABLE and related emotional literacy topics
- Running workshops for parents in the ENABLE approach so they could support the behaviour management strategies at home
- Training key staff in the conduct of parent interviews to support effective assessment of the children and all staff in extension activities for the emotionally able and talented children
- Provision of in depth supervision with the Learning Support Staff working with individual children and supervision for teaching staff regarding behaviour management strategies
- Guidance on the development of confidentiality and safe touch policies and school action to address the five national outcomes for children set out in the Children Act 2004

Marnie, aged 5, was behaving in ways that caused staff concern. It was difficult to contain her in the classroom. She was unkempt and looked physically not well cared for. She was very agitated, had difficulty concentrating and had no friends. She was always restless, unable to sit still. She would run around with her head down avoiding eye contact. An ENABLE assessment of her behaviours which included being out of touch with her own needs; fear of sudden change and separation; storming ahead or dragging behind; lack of empathy for others; poor relationships with peer group; and saying 'no' and 'I won't' in many

(Continued)

circumstances, suggested that her emotional development had been interrupted at a very early stage (Learning to Be). Marnie needed to learn the basics of being in a safe, trusting relationship. Adults had to anticipate and meet her needs and to keep her safe at all times. An action plan was drawn up so that all of the staff involved with Marnie were aware of how to be with her and what to do to ensure she had the experiences she needed to do the missed emotional learning. Marnie joined a group of eight children to do reparative play work with a trained ENABLE co-ordinator and a learning support assistant. In addition, she had a half-hour one-to-one session once a week. All staff were also invited to make the best possible use of their contacts with Marnie by looking at her, responding with warmth and tolerance, sharing joy and enjoyment of being in a relationship with her and responding positively to her signals for attention most of the time. Within the one-to-one work, the co-ordinator played eye games with Marnie in an attempt to bring her into a relationship. This was built on in the small group with peek-a-boo games, and projects on eyes, which included:

■ Looking at eyes in mirrors
■ Drawing and painting eyes
■ Photographing eyes
■ Games with facial expressions using eyes.

Marnie really responded quickly. She developed a strong bond with the co-ordinator first and then fairly quickly with her classroom teacher. Her behaviour calmed, she was more able to concentrate, she developed friendships with other children and became much happier.

Two years on, it was reported, 'On a recent visit to the school, she came skipping over to me, head up and smiling to greet me. This project has helped the girl to grow so that she can attach to others; she has developed empathy and she is learning'. Evidence from the qualitative evaluation of ENABLE, as well as quantitative data has shown that the approach and the computer software package has had an impact on:

■ Children's attainment – children within the programme made improvements (beyond expectation) in National Curriculum assessments in maths, reading and writing
■ Children's emotional health and well-being demonstrated by their interactions with peers and adults and their class based behaviour as well as, in some cases, their relationships at home
■ Teachers' confidence in developing positive strategies for dealing with children whose behaviour they find difficult to manage
■ Support staffs' ability and confidence in promoting children's emotional and social development
■ Parents' engagement with the school and their commitment to children's learning
■ The school ethos and relationships throughout the school

Following this pilot project South Brent is committed to continuing the ENABLE approach. Head teacher, Helen Nicholls says, 'It has liberated our school to do what is right for children so that all staff are free to meet children's needs for quality teacher–learner

(Continued)

(Continued)

relationships and improved curriculum provision. In so doing, the children have been phenomenally successful academically and socially. ENABLE gave us the understanding of children's development to be able to contribute positively to children's emotional learning. It provided a model and an approach that expanded staff skills in working with challenging children and in so doing has improved staff morale – and it gave us a framework for accountability which has given the work with children credibility.'

The implications of brain research for learning

As Katherine Weare noted in her editorial for *Health Education*:

> *Many engaged in education have traditionally taken the view that students' feelings about their learning are irrelevant to how well they do at the task in hand. Some have even thought that students learn better when stressed, humiliated, anxious and under pressure. New research on how the brain works is showing that the opposite is in fact the case and that a positive emotional state is a crucial prerequisite for learning. When a person is under stress – fear, anxiety, and anger – the upper, more sophisticated parts of the brain more or less shut down …*
>
> *It follows that we need to pay attention to the emotional state of the learner, and to ensure that they are not stressed or feeling under threat, if we want them to learn anything. We need to recognise and help prevent the emotional states that can block learning … (Weare, 2004: 5)*

The emotionally confident child, young person or adult is authentically who they are and has an aliveness, vitality, energy and a sense of inquiry. They are full of excitement and passion for people, for things and for learning. These people get back up again when they fall down. Things have to happen in the brain before we can do this. The child's brain development is supported through positive care and relationship, through offering boundaries and consistency. Some of the children and young people whose boundaries have been violated by different types of neglect and abuse are our major challenges. We need to try and get those boundaries back and help children and young people respect them through consistent, fair and planned support.

We must put the emotional and social development of the child at the heart of the learning process if we are interested in supporting the love of learning. Doing this will have implications for every aspect of school life, from simple everyday interactions – like the way people and children are welcomed into the school – to the way the whole school responds to crises and shocks – like the way staff handle bereavement or violent incidents. Good head teachers and their staff teams stand at the school gates at the beginning of the school day and welcome people in. They really notice them all, making eye contact and being interested in them. Adults who are interested in children listen to them; they want to know how the children are experiencing the world. They also ask questions, which are relevant, pertinent and sometimes informed by previous information so the child believes they really matter and feel important. Even though this is easier in smaller primary schools, large secondary schools also need to find and maximise ways to create a sense of belonging and mattering for all of their pupils.

Because of the size of secondary schools, many have found that the emotional health and well-being needs of young people are best attended to if the school is organised into smaller sections. Pastoral and welfare support needs are then attended to through these smaller groups. This only works if real attention is paid to the process of making smaller sections work so that young people feel special and valued, as well as confident, and there is someone they can talk to and get help and advice from.

Wider school processes that contribute to this include:

- How children and young people are involved in decision-making

- Whether parents and carers are welcomed and supported to engage with the school and their child's education

- How the positive attitudes of all staff members towards children and young people are demonstrated and reflected in their behaviour towards them

When children feel contained, valued and cared for, when they are inspired and encouraged, when they are supported to succeed and challenged to extend themselves and they know their efforts are seen and appreciated, then they want to learn and to develop themselves in as many ways as possible. This desire to develop themselves is crucial, as McLaughlin and Alexander state:

> The construction of the passive learner soaking up knowledge does not fit with what we now know about learning. The need to deal with the explosion of knowledge and the necessary reconfiguration of how we approach teaching and learning requires change in schools. The aims of the curriculum should be to develop students who can work co-operatively, with initiative, independence, perseverance and flexibility; who can move easily in the emotional domain; who can communicate effectively; tolerate ambiguity; reason sensibly; plan and solve problems; who can obtain and use information; learn how to learn; evaluate themselves and others; possess perseverance; tolerate difference and have an ability to work in multicultural settings. These elements are to be found in much current work on learning and curriculum development. Claxton (1999) calls them the three Rs of learning power – resilience, resourcefulness and reflectiveness. All these approaches draw on what we know about learning – that it is actively constructed, situationally specific, complex, hard to transfer and encouraged by social forces. They also show that the development of the personal, social and emotional is central to the development of learning and achievement. (McLaughlin and Alexander, 2004: 18)

The importance of relationships

> When a baby is first born, the 'mummy' is in a bit of a fog and the baby is working it out. When it goes well there is a strong attachment and an 'in love ness' of the 'mother' and baby. Through the process of the loving relationship the baby's neurones join up. It is through the little noises, breaths and acknowledging of the baby that the baby's brain is beginning to come alive. It begins to understand and learn in the beautiful dance of relationship. And the neuronal pathways join up and join up – ping ping. (Bird, 2006)

Positive emotional and social development is most reliant on the development of strong relationships between adults and children and the promotion of relationships amongst peers. As young people involved in Getting It Together told us: 'We want adults who understand that the way they treat us in everyday life affects our confidence, our self-esteem and our emotional health. We don't want to be treated like children, but don't expect us to be adults either.'

Child development experts such as Stern (1985) assert that we develop a sense of self through our relationships with others, through shared experiences and the feedback we receive from these experiences. Crucially the experience of being in a positive relationship is a process that helps children and young people to develop empathy and understanding about the impact of their actions on others and a sense of responsibility for this.

Teaching about relationships and supporting the development of relationship skills is important, but insufficient alone. The greatest learning takes place through the experience of being in relationships with others. Working with different people, in different ways, and being encouraged to take on different roles within these experiences and reflect on what happened, helps us truly learn about ourselves. We learn by experiencing, we learn by doing and we learn by reflecting on those experiences. We need to give and receive feedback from others about our impact and about our behaviours. When this is supportive, constructive and focused on learning we evolve and develop ourselves. We learn about what works in one-to-one situations as well as what works and does not work in small and large groups. We learn about when and where we are personally comfortable or uncomfortable and how to manage these feelings and keep ourselves 'in the moment'. We also learn to recognise that we have choices about how we behave.

Through positive relationships children develop empathy, trust, perseverance, independence and interdependence. With these helpful experiences they develop the skills to participate actively, to work with peers and adults, to dream, set themselves challenges and strategies to achieve them, as well as regulate their behaviour. Strong and reparative relationships with a worker are particularly important for those children who have not formed strong attachments with a carer in the early years (further information about working with vulnerable children and young people is on page 28).

This is why it is crucial that teachers and support staff spend time getting to know children and young people as individuals, learning their likes and their dislikes, their joys, hopes, aspirations and talents, and forming effective relationships, demonstrating they care and are interested. In the award-winning fiction book, *We've got to talk about Kevin*, by Lionel Shriver, in one of the letters to her estranged husband, Eva talks about how children can smell the 'inauthentic' and see when they are given a pat sentence, rather than a caring comment. And this is borne out in the everyday reality of working with children and young people. They regularly talk about the teacher 'who cared', the learning mentor who was 'really interested' and single out as uninspiring and poor those who 'didn't bother to get to know your name or anything about you', or 'didn't listen and just made assumptions'.

In the *Heart of a Teacher*, Britton (1998) describes her experience of asking students to explain what makes a good teacher. Again, it is the quality of the relationship that is important:

> As I listen to these stories, it becomes impossible to claim that all good teachers use similar techniques: some lecture non-stop and others speak very little, some stay close to their material and others involve imagination, some teach with the carrot and others with the stick. But in every story, I have heard, good teachers share one trait: a strong sense of identity infuses their work. Dr A is really there when he teaches me …

Building relationships takes time, attention and a willingness to 'hang on in there' in the face of frequent rebuffs or rejection from children and young people. In a real relationship we react differently to situations, depending on a whole range of factors: our mood, our sense of what the child or young person needs today and the reasons underpinning their behaviours, the need to change the emotional tone of the exchange and so forth. Children and young people need to meet us as a real person so the most important qualities to bring to the relationship are self-awareness, humility, compassion, understanding and our particular style.

Because the experience of being in relationships and reflecting on these relationships is central to emotional development, the *process* of working in groups and ensuring effective assessment *for* learning are important learning processes. Working as a group enables exploration of new roles and ways of being, and assessment for learning potentially helping people to move from cognitive understanding to assimilating the cognitive and emotional interrelationship which can affect or change their future behaviours.

Children and young people also need role models who they can observe and emulate, as well as opportunities to practise ways of being and behaving. Regular planned opportunities such as free and structured play, music, art, drama and creativity, group work and circle time help them to learn about themselves and their personalities, and to develop successful interactions with others. Young people welcome the chance to explore feelings and values within structured exercises like those in the *Cards for Life* pack (NCB, 2005). Older students benefit from opportunities to devise and implement community action programmes. See Changemakers and the materials from the Active Citizens in Schools Project *The ACIS KnowHow Pack* (DfES, 2005).

A fundamental aspect of emotional literacy is the ability to name and accurately describe emotions. Having an emotional vocabulary is essential if we want to enable children and young people to be able to manage their feelings and think when they are feeling, and before they act, so they are able to behave positively. There are lots of words to describe feelings, even though many of us restrict ourselves to a very limited vocabulary and all of us will use language differently to describe what we feel.

As a role model you can use a positive language of different emotions – being careful to distinguish between strength of emotion such as feeling happy and feeling elated, and helping children and young people you are working with recognise the subtle differences. Use images to help with the distinctions. Where suitable in different situations, offer children and young people words to help them describe what they are feeling. Be careful never to enforce a feeling, but offer feeling words or images and allow them to choose and describe, to ask for clarification or to find their own word.

In practice

On a training course a primary teacher described how they had made very determined efforts to improve the emotionality of the class through offering feelings words. When investigating a playground incident she was talking to one boy and he was describing how he understood the incident. When asking him how he felt when he was being excluded from the games in the playground she offered him a range of feeling words including angry, jealous, sad and lonely. She gave him time to reflect and when he did not respond she said, 'You know sometimes I feel like I am going to explode when I feel left out or if people are being unfair'. He excitedly started describing how he felt like he was being stirred around inside and different bits of his tummy felt like they were being stirred like a wizard stirs a cauldron.

They went on from here to discuss what this feeling was caused by and to develop successful strategies for resolving the incident. She has since successfully used visual descriptions as a way of helping children to describe how they are feeling.

Being an effective role model for children and young people's emotional development

- Be prepared to develop authentic positive relationships and demonstrate you care and are interested

- Model the behaviours you hope to encourage in children and young people, including self-awareness and the ability to manage and express emotions as well as talk about them

- Praise and reward those behaviours which are helpful and important

- Be genuine and authentic including saying when behaviours upset you

- Demonstrate excitement, passion and wonder for new things, ideas and learning

- Look beyond behaviours and develop empathic responses

- Be fun and playful

- Demonstrate respect for difference and diversity, and ensure that prejudice and discrimination does not go unchallenged (Bird and Gerlach, 2005)

The impact of effective relationship

A research study found the single most effective factor in helping young people feel more mature, confident, informed, sensitive and respectful of cultural, social and sexual difference was the quality of the relationship they had with their teacher. They said their teacher was 'good at giving them the opportunity to ask questions, was very open and patient … just a good man. He did not teach straight from books and was willing to use real experiences to explain things and to help you. He was respectful whatever their opinions. He never laughed at us'.

The students reported that he 'made us think about men in a different way'. ('Evaluation of sex and relationship education with Year 9 pupils in Newham schools', cited in Gerlach and Bird, 1999.)

Showing we care

Some people feel worried about children or young people giving information and asking for confidential help. As a result there are many professionals who have said in a range of fora that if someone asks if they can talk to me, I tell them: 'I can't promise that I can keep everything confidential. There are some things I am duty bound to tell.'

Describing how a child had asked if she could tell her a secret, one worker said, I replied, 'As you know I care about you and so I am happy to listen to you. But if I was really worried that something terrible was happening or might happen we might need to get some help. But I wouldn't do anything without talking to you about it first.'

In both the same message is being conveyed, but the latter demonstrates care and concern for the child in a way which will increase confidence.

Building emotional resilience

A key task of early childhood is building emotional resilience. As the child experiences being soothed and calmed by their primary carer when distressed, they develop the internal brain and body mechanisms to be able to soothe themselves and so to manage stress for themselves as they get older. The adult helps the child to regulate their emotions. If this has not happened sufficiently before the child comes to school, then the child needs to have these containing, calming, soothing and regulating experiences with a significant adult. Once the child does feel safe, special and like they belong and matter, the neuronal pathways in their brain will begin to redesign stress management systems that allow more access to thinking. Blocks and obstacles become challenges and not barriers.

The evidence suggests there are fundamental building blocks to building resilience. These are:

■ A secure base, whereby the child feels a sense of belonging and security and can develop good self-esteem – an internal sense of worth and competence

■ A sense of self-efficacy, that is, a sense of mastery and control, along with an accurate understanding of personal strengths and limitations

To develop this resilience there are some key life skills that schools can help children develop through specific activities and opportunities as well as through their relationships. These include:

■ Having a sense of optimism and possibilities

■ Being self-aware and able to learn and develop from their experiences

■ Managing risk-taking and coping with the outcomes

■ Celebrating individual and group successes

■ Being able to ask for help

■ Taking care of one's own emotional and physical needs

■ Developing empathy

■ Managing loss

Just as children learn different skills from supervised and free play, children and young people need both to be able to take risks with and without appropriate supervision – as appropriate – and learn from the consequences.

There are times within school that it may be helpful for children and young people to be able to work through the risk they are about to take, find ways of managing the risk, and then coping with the outcome. By doing this without adult intervention, children can learn directly from their experience – mistakes included. In turn this helps them learn to co-operate with others, giving and getting help as needed. It also builds self-confidence and emotional resilience as a child learns to manage their 'successes' and 'failures' and can pick up the pieces again undaunted if necessary.

Meeting children's needs

This section first summarises what all children need to promote their emotional and social development, and then focuses specifically on the needs of vulnerable children and young people in schools. It then offers practical ideas for responding appropriately.

Table 2.1 What all children need

What children need	How schools offer this
To be and to feel safe	Through having strong policies and practices on issues relating to safety including activities developing emotional competence through PSHE; anti-bullying and behaviour management practices and the provision of positive playground activities and strong pastoral systems Through being known and valued by adults Through having a 'safe haven': a space that is yours and a contact member of staff that looks out for you
To have their basic needs recognised such as • Hunger and thirst • Comfort • Privacy • Things that are needed	These basic needs are addressed through routines such as breakfast clubs and fruit schemes, provision of good quality lunches (and positive ways of encouraging free school lunch take up such as swipe cards where relevant). Easy access to water is an important aid to learning, as the brain needs to be re-hydrated regularly. Comfort needs are attended to through provision of quiet spaces and sofas for people to read on or rest Privacy can be provided through having a coat hook or a locker, which is their own, and, where possible, places to go where they can be on their own. Pens, pencils, note pads, uniforms can all be provided by the school for those children and young people whose circumstances mean they are not able to get these things elsewhere
Knowing you matter and somebody is interested in you	Ensuring there is a commitment to recognising children and young people as individuals. As form tutors or class teachers, asking questions, following up conversation and responding to particular incidents well. A strong pastoral care system must also be in place that children and young people know about and have confidence in accessing *A form tutor in the North East makes sure that when Year 7 pupils first arrive in her form she spends enough time with each pupil over the first term to find out a bit about their lives. She then follows up in a cyclical fashion on any special interests or areas of difficulty individuals may have. She also makes the pupils aware that they can come and talk to her at any time to get help with a difficult situation or to find out about something that interests them*
Having specialness and uniqueness nurtured and valued	Schools can provide opportunities to identify the interests, talents and skills of children and through school and community based partnerships and valued experiences provide opportunities for them to develop their interests and skills The consistent attention to providing positive and constructive feedback enables children and young people to learn, as well as the use of suitable broad-based rewards systems within school
Stimulating and attractive environments	Using bright paper, colourful work and interesting material for displays on the wall

Table 2.1 (Continued)	
What children need	How schools offer this
Curiosity ignited	A pupil referral unit in London laminates a 'feeling word' of the week and its meaning and posts them in different places around the PRU. Tutors take time to discuss the words in different classes and they have noticed a stronger interest in words and improved vocabulary over a period of time
Opportunities to be in relationships that are used consciously to promote emotional development	Through a stimulating curriculum that is active, relevant for their stage of development, maturity and interests and that is structured to relate to the individual needs of children and young people
	This can be through class and form teacher, classroom or teaching assistants, support staff, dinner supervisors, learning mentors, peer support processes, special activity groups at lunchtime or before and after school. Relationships can also be nurtured through the school journey, for example through walking buses
Opportunities to participate in decision-making	Children and young people can participate in decision-making in a range of ways including school councils, class councils, interviewing staff and policy development or healthy schools groups. Active Citizenship provides opportunities for decision-making in the wider school community
Opportunities to learn about cause and effect and to problem-solve	Provided for through free and supervised play enabling children and young people to take risks and learn from them, through active learning in the classroom for example in Sports or Science, through processing learning from experiences and through promoting skills for conflict resolution
To recognise and talk about feelings and to learn to think whilst feeling something strongly	This takes place through planned activities in Personal, Social and Health Education, or through stress, anxiety and anger management classes. It is an important aspect of all opportunities for students to reflect on their learning in all subjects. It also takes place through effective facilitation of conflict when it occurs between children and young people
To learn to get along with others and adopt a range of different roles	With careful attention this happens through everyday classroom interactions. In order to be successful staff will need to think about the range of groupings and experiences that children and young people are provided with and encouraged to participate in. It also takes place through planned provision for learning about teams, groups and leadership roles for example in circle time, within initiatives and in Personal, Social Health Education and Citizenship

Meeting the needs of vulnerable children and young people

The challenge for us, is to go really deep with these (vulnerable) children and young people, to spend the time building the relationships, find out what they need and what will help them to develop new ways of thinking, of being and of doing. Unless we do this, all our efforts to improve learning, and achieve public health targets such as sexual health, teenage pregnancy and substance misuse will be meaningless, lost in the wilderness of young people's worlds, where they are not choosing not to look after themselves, but rather they don't know how to. (Bird, 2006)

A significant number of children and young people are going to school on a daily basis having experienced or experiencing abuse, violence and neglect. Schools are a 'safety net' for many of these children and young people, by offering different ways to be and to experience the world. Staff need to become significant to these pupils, building trusting relationships with them as well as providing developmentally appropriate experiences in age-appropriate ways. In this way pupils can be supported to do the emotional learning they need in ways that do not expose or humiliate them. This helps vulnerable students to develop self-confidence and a range of emotional and social skills, so that they can make best use of the support services that are available. Schools can be key to providing the one-to-one advice and help that may prove to be a virtual, if not actual, lifeline.

This is not an easy challenge. It is for this reason that strong effective partnerships are absolutely crucial. Schools best provide specialist support and the range of reparative experiences that are necessary in partnership with behaviour specialists, as well as those in health and the voluntary sector. Ignoring the increasing numbers of emotionally damaged children who are entering schools is not an option.

Emotions hinder learning or promote it. Facilitating pupils' emotional capacity is key to engaging them in more effective learning so that they become creative, competent contributors to a thriving community and wider global society. The Extended and Healthy Schools Programmes provide vital mechanisms for developing the partnerships.

> In one local authority in England with high levels of deprivation, the local authority adviser estimated that many schools have as many as 50 per cent of children in their classes who needed some level of intensive support that could not be provided without significant partnerships with a range of professionals.

Understanding children's needs and responding appropriately

There is a range of behaviours, which children and young people who are emotionally damaged display. Unfortunately there is no single set of behaviours and no two people will respond in the same way to the same situations. How they behave will depend upon their personalities, their emotional resourcefulness and how people have responded to them in the past.

Again this emphasises why the relationship between an adult and individual children and young people is so important. Adults need to learn to understand behaviours within the context of individual personalities and experiences. For example, a child who is noisy or disruptive in class may well be behaving in response to the lesson content, or being reminded of a particular life event or situation. Another child who experiences similar circumstances may be withdrawn or inattentive.

The increasing numbers of support staff in school (as long as they are well trained and supported with significant influence) is particularly helpful as they often have a greater amount of time available to them for one-to-one work and relationship-building than teacher do. This enables the development of strong relationships and an opportunity to understand what the child or young person's behaviours are telling us.

The evidence shows that children and young people who are emotionally damaged may demonstrate a wide range of behaviours to 'protect themselves'. These behaviours include:

- Denial, excuses, forgetting and contradicting

- Distracting or changing topics of conversation

- Being passive, showing anger and avoiding eye contact

- Minimising or controlling

- Dissociating or avoiding

- Challenging boundaries and rules

- Chattering or mumbling

- Repetitive movements, fidgeting, rigid body or scratching

- Defiance or vagueness

- Masking, repressing or denying feelings

- Blaming, arguing or lying

- Obsessions and creating obsessive rituals

- Somatisation (feeling unwell)

- Damaging or defacing work

Resources like the ENABLE computer program can assist adults working with vulnerable children to assess the needs underlying their worrying behaviours. Children may react to situations that generate emotional discomfort in a variety of ways, none of which actually solve the problem or deal with the issue that confronts them. These include ways that are

- Distracting or diverting of the energy like behaving in an agitated manner

- Violent or aggressive so that the energy is used against others or themselves

- Incapacitating so the situation is avoided or has to stop

- People-pleasing and over-adaptive so that attention is focused on others

- Refusals, covert or overt, where the energy is channelled into doing nothing or as little as possible

Understanding each group of behaviours helps the adult to select a way of responding to the behaviour in ways that will help the child to learn what they need to do next to manage their emotions better. Importantly, these practical strategies need to take place in the context of a caring, boundaried relationship. The success of strategies that are adopted will depend upon the quality of the relationship that exists, as well as the adult's capacity for self-regulation and creativity. Hughes (2002) lists a number of helpful responses to troubling behaviours. He recommends adopting an attitude described within the acronym PACE:

- Playful

- Accepting

- Curious

- Empathic

He maintains that the adult needs to set the emotional tone for any exchange. Above all, the adult needs to stay emotionally regulated so that they themselves, are not pulled into 'acting out' or displaying defensive behaviours.

Supporting transition

A transition is a change from one state or phase of life to another, or a change of circumstances. Transitions occur throughout our lives, and all children and young people face many transitions as they move through puberty, adolescence and into adulthood (Worthy, 2005). Some transitions will be expected and there is the potential to plan for these, for example the move from primary school to secondary school. Some transitions and critical moments occur that are not foreseen and therefore are less easy to plan for, such as bereavement or separation from family through being placed in public care. Some of the transitions that children and young people go through are:

- Starting a new school

- Moving school

- Puberty

- Bereavement

- Parents separating

- Illness (their own, a parent or a sibling)

- Changing friendship groups

- Entry to, or leaving a pupil referral unit

■ Moving through child health services into adult services

■ Coming out as gay or lesbian

■ Leaving home

Well-developed emotional resilience is key to children and young people effectively moving through both the expected and unexpected transitions they face.

Developing the skills and qualities needed for life's challenges is a necessary journey that we all need to make throughout our lives. We can prepare children and young people for some of those challenges, others are unexpected and therefore must be managed as they occur. Children and young people can be supported in many practical ways as they make their own way in the world, and all those who work with them need to understand their needs and how they can meet them.

Ten principles for supporting effective transitions

In times of transition there is a need for information, emotional support, practical help and resources. An individual worker's role will vary in ensuring this can be put in place, depending on circumstances and the nature of the transition. Below are some questions and 10 principles to help you think about how best to support children and young people through their transitions.

Consider the principles below in the light of the following questions:

■ What critical moments or transitions might the children or young people you are working with face?

■ What help or support would be useful to them at different stages?

■ Are there any 'special' circumstances facing them? For example, are they looked after, do they have a disability, or have they suffered bereavement?

■ What training or support do you need to help them?

■ In thinking about these questions have you considered the transitions and critical moments that face a small percentage of pupils within every school, such as refugee and asylum-seeking children and looked after children?

Ten Principles for supporting effective transitions

1   Identify key changes, critical moments and transition points for children and young people, including those most children will experience, such as moving school, and those that some children will experience, such as family break-up or bereavement, and ensure the relevant people are aware of the impact of change and the importance of support through transition.

2   Ensure mainstream work with children and young people builds life skills, including emotional resilience and empathy, and emphasises the importance of asking for help and support when they are needed.

3   Develop curriculum and project work that focuses on transitions and helps children and young people understand the range of transitions they will experience as they move from puberty, through adolescence and into adulthood.

4   Prepare children and young people for leaving school or leaving care well in advance, providing an opportunity to reflect on successes and challenges and celebrate their work together.

5   Identify individuals who may need particular support through transitions. Identify the support mechanisms and agencies that are available for the child and their family. Work in partnership to provide this support, where possible.

6   Involve children and young people in providing support to their peers as part of every-day friendships and relationships. This can be developed as peer support.

7   Involve and support parents and carers in transitions work so they can celebrate the transitions and provide understanding and support.

8   Encourage optimism and work with the excitement and opportunities, as well as the fears and anxieties caused by change and transitions.

9   If the behaviour of a child or young person changes, encourage them to acknowledge it and talk about it. Are there issues relating to transition and change that are causing difficulties and what can be done to address these?

10   Provide consistent responses to critical moments and events in children and young people's lives, such as when they are bullied, bereaved or experiencing parental divorce or separation. Ensure the child is at the heart of deciding what support and help they need. Discuss with a child when they are happy for their peers and others to know and understand what has happened, and who they would like to tell them.

Making the move from primary to secondary: a carnival parade

In a primary school in Dewsbury, West Yorkshire, a carnival parade marks the transition of pupils from primary to secondary school, and is one aspect of Roots and Wings, a Children's Fund project.

In July 2005, in the last week of term the whole of Year 6 went for a walk, each sporting a set of wings painted on the back of a T-shirt. They invited their friends, families, school and folk from the community to follow them on a short but momentous journey. They carried the sculptures they had made over the past few weeks, each representing a quality they felt would be needed when they reached their destination – the local secondary school where most would be taking a place in the new term. Their sculptures included The Pyramid of Happiness, The Cottage of Strong Friendship, The Lighthouse Towers of Confidence, The Triumphant Castle of Achievement, The Igloo of Enjoyment and Eiffel Ben, Tower of Proudness.

The mayor and her consort were there. The children had crafted formal invitations printed on golden paper. They had written press releases and briefed every other class in their school as to the meaning of the event. Some of the children had worked with musicians, made drums and percussion instruments and formed a street band for the event. They led every-one in singing the chant they had composed: 'We're going up, we're going up, we're going up together.'

Leaving the school grounds, the parade was met by the whole school, friends, family and locals lining the road, cheering and waving home-made windmills and fans. Community police officers ensured that traffic stopped. It was important that the children claimed the streets and not the pavements. Folk came out of their houses and shops to wave. Half an hour later and the parade was approaching the secondary school.

Year 7 was out in force at the secondary school, lining the long drive leading to the main entrance. Some of them had taken part in the first parade the year before. One of the mothers commented: 'He came home and told me they had to line up when the parade came to school. "You get out there and clap and cheer", I told him. 'Remember how you felt last year"'.

The parade had to narrow down to walk through the young people, clapping, shouting and encouraging them forward. Senior staff from the secondary school were waiting at the entrance. Everyone – and their sculptures – was ushered into the school hall. There, mounted on the walls at ceiling height, were the structures from the previous year's event.

The ritual was established last year. This is the moment when the primary head teacher hands over garlands of origami birds, symbolising the children, and asks the secondary school to please take care of them. This year, before taking the garlands, the secondary head talked of the young people's skills and talents, how they are capable of so many things, of how they are people in their own right.

Some of the young people who had been 'handed over' last year talked of their experience at high school since, and invited the younger pupils to join in wholeheartedly. In 2005 the

(Continued)

(Continued)

mayor spoke too. She felt she had to, she said, because she had walked the walk and felt the warmth and emotion of the parade hard on her heels. One of the children, aged 11, commented: 'This project makes the community into one big family. It is a tradition. When you are part of it, it makes you feel special.'

KEY POINTS

- Addressing the emotional and social development of young people is crucial for learning, health and inclusion

- All children and young people need to learn how to use their feelings and thinking skills to guide their behaviour positively. Some will need additional targeted support

- There are a number of developmental 'tasks' that all children and young people must go through — many will need these revisited if they have not been 'achieved' earlier in their lives

CHAPTER 3

Getting started: a whole-school approach

This chapter sets out practical strategies for promoting emotional and social development in schools. It explores;

- The importance of a whole-school approach
- Supporting staff emotional health and well-being
- Effective policy development
- Participation of children and young people
- Partnerships with the range of community partners

To be effective and have the maximum impact, the promotion of emotional health and well-being needs to be seen as a whole-setting issue, where policies, procedures and all those in an institution work towards the same goal. The National Healthy Schools Programme has identified 10 elements for the development of an effective whole-school approach (NHSS, 2004):

- Leadership, management and managing change

- Policy development

- Curriculum planning and resourcing

- Teaching and learning

- Culture and environment

- Giving children and young a voice

- Provision of support services

- Staff professional development needs, health and welfare

- Partnerships with parents, carers and the community

- Assessing, recording and reporting achievement

Antidote – the campaign for emotional literacy – offers the following guiding principles for the development of a strategic approach.

1   Start by exploring what things really feel like for the people in place, taking time to understand what is working well and what seems to be causing difficulty.
2   Seek out the empathy and creativity within the school and find ways to build on existing work, rather than diverting energy to an entirely new initiative.
3   Collaborate with staff and students to develop new ways of working in response to their interests and needs.
4   Use every opportunity for ongoing reflection with leadership, staff and students, evaluating and celebrating the work as it evolves.
5   Ask and keep asking: What's going on here? What does it feel like? What might make it feel better?

Getting started

You are not starting with a blank sheet. Within your school there will be much existing good practice, some successes to build on and some challenges or experiences to learn from and perhaps avoid. Getting started is all about identifying what the needs are within your school community and how to set about meeting these needs. Often when people start to audit their work they recognise how much they are already doing and the expertise that already exists.

The questions in the audit tool/checklist are designed to help you with the auditing process:

Policy	How will you know you have achieved it?	Possible evidence for Healthy School Status or Ofsted inspection	Areas for development	Timescale
Has a named member of staff responsible for PSHE provision with sufficient status, training and appropriate senior management support within the school		• Named SMT support within school • School CPD file referring to PSHE		
Has up-to-date policies in place – developed through wide consultation (e.g. with children, parents, staff, governors, school-partners), implemented and monitored and evaluated for impact – which are owned, understood and implemented by the whole-school community including children and young people.		• Pupils, parents/carers and staff know and understand the bullying policy		
Covering:		• Child protection policy in line with Area Child Protection Committee that has been approved by the governors		
Anti-bullying		• Confidentiality policy that is known and understood by pupils, parents and staff and has been approved by the governors		
Child protection		• Managing drugs-related incidents policy in line with DfES guidance that is known and understood by pupils, parents and staff and has been approved by the governors. This policy should contain a range of sanctions and measures for supporting pupils who may need help in managing drug issues		
Confidentiality		• SRE policy in place that is known and understood by the pupils, the parents and the staff, and has been approved by the governors. It will contain information on the supportive measures that are in place in the case of any pupil's unplanned pregnancy		
Drugs		• A survey has been taken of the whole of the school site, involving children, to identify any areas where children and or staff or visitors feel unsafe. These areas have been improved, e.g. with lighting, landscaping and/or staffing		
Sex and relationships Safety and site security		• The policy directs attention to the need to provide opportunities for every child to experience success and for these successes to be acknowledged. Adults understand the need for a few simple, easily understood rules, clarity about boundaries and consistency in their application		
Rewards and sanctions Ofsted self-evaluation 2a, 4a, 4b, 4c, 4d, 4e				

Policy	How will you know you have achieved it?	Possible evidence for Healthy School Status or Ofsted inspection	Areas for development	Timescale
Identifies vulnerable individuals and groups and establishes appropriate strategies to support them and their families		• SEN policy • Inclusion policy • Routes of referral • System for identification • Pupil tracking system • Named staff member liaises with parents and children out of school • Buddying, mentoring and coaching systems offer support for the most vulnerable and also provide ways for vulnerable children to take responsibility and shine		
Provides clear leadership to create and manage a positive environment which enhances emotional health and well-being in school - including the management of the behaviour and rewards policies Ofsted self-evaluation 4a, 4b, 4c		• School self-evaluation form • School development plan • Discussion with head teacher and PSHE co-ordinator • Relevant policies, e.g. behaviour and rewards policy • The head teacher and senior management team offer good role models through their respectful, emotionally intelligent behaviour • All staff are expected to interact with children positively • All staff are expected – and supported through school procedures and systems – to model emotionally intelligent behaviour		
Has mechanisms in place to ensure all pupils' views are reflected in curriculum planning, teaching and learning and the whole-school environment, including those with special educational needs and specific health conditions, as well as disaffected pupils, young carers and teenage parents Ofsted self-evaluation 2a, 2b,		• Teaching and learning policy • School inclusion policy • Pupils' views • Staff are aware of pupils' learning styles on a group basis and, for vulnerable children, on an individual basis so that learning tasks can be provided at levels that invite, encourage and extend learning with ample room for success		

Participation and partnership	How will you know you have achieved it?	Possible evidence	Areas for development	Timescale
Provides opportunities for pupils to participate to build their confidence and self-esteem Ofsted self-evaluation 4b		• Programmes of study/schemes of work • Celebrations • Behaviour and rewards policy • Learning and teaching policy • Pupils' views		
		• Processes, procedures and programmes that address the needs of the vulnerable and challenging children to ensure they are supported to contribute and engage in social and community - based initiatives		
Involves professionals from appropriate external agencies to create specialist teams to support PSHE delivery and to improve skills and knowledge, such as a school nurse, sexual health outreach workers and drug education advisers Ofsted self-evaluation 4a		• Schemes of work reflect appropriate use of outside agencies • Policy or guidelines about how to use external visitors • Staff involved in teaching PSHE understand how their relationships with children, and the way they construct opportunities for the development of positive interactions between children, contribute significantly to children's emotional health and well-being – and they act on this understanding		
Has a confidential pastoral support system in place for pupils and staff to access advice, especially at times of bereavement and other major life changes and that this system actively works to combat stigma and discrimination Ofsted self-evaluation 4b		• Pupils understand the pastoral system • Identified route for referral for staff and pupils • Child protection policy (ref 1.5) • Inclusion policy • Examples of good practice in combating stigma and discrimination • Identified support structure for children identified with emotional developmental needs and/or behavioural difficulties		

Figure 3.1 Emotional health and well-being: audit tool/check list for schools

 Photocopiable: Promoting Emotional and Social Development in Schools
Paul Chapman Publishing © 2007 Simon Blake with Julia Bird and Lynne Gerlach

Once the audit is completed through discussion with colleagues, including the senior management team (SMT), the next stage is to develop an action plan, which is realistic and visionary, positive and pragmatic. In establishing an action plan it is helpful to remember having a long-term plan with clearly defined small steps will encourage success. As you complete and see the positive impact of achieving small steps you will feel more confident and proud, making it likely you and your colleagues will continue, being braver and bolder as you go along. If you start with too many actions which are not achievable with the time and resources available, it is likely you will become disillusioned and less will be achieved in the longer term.

Antidote provides an online self-evaluation tool (School Emotional Environment for Learning Survey – SEELS) which provides information to help start improving the emotional environment of your class or school. SEELS works by:

■ Measuring a school's emotional environment for learning

■ Diagnosing the factors that need addressing to improve that environment

■ Identifying the main levers for change

■ Tracking changes through time

Visit www.antidote.org.uk to find out more.

Developing an effective policy framework

Any practice development requires emotional health and well-being to be addressed at a strategic whole-school policy level. Some schools integrate emotional health and well-being issues across their policies. Others have a specific policy addressing how the school intends to promote emotional well-being.

Both have their benefits, however it is only through true integration that emotional health and well-being will take centre stage in the life of the school as it rightly should. An increasing number of schools are preparing a statement of intent with regard to the promotion of emotional health and well-being. This identifies in which policies there is specific reference to emotional health and well-being.

The process of developing a policy or a statement of intent is at least as important, if not more important, than actually having one. As with all policy development, it needs to be done in a positive and emotionally literate way. In summary this means:

■ Ensuring that children, young people and their families have opportunities to contribute and that active efforts are made to seek a range of views across the spectrum of perspectives within the school

■ Ensuring the staff team has opportunities to provide its ideas and views and identify existing successes and areas for development

■ Ensuring that all those involved in the policy development and review process have a chance to discuss both their thoughts and their feelings about existing practice and opportunities for development

■ Using language which everyone understands so the whole-school community can understand how it applies to them

■ Ensuring that adequate time and resources are allocated to the development and implementation of the policy

Staff emotional health and well-being

Looking after the emotional health and well-being of staff is as crucial as looking after that of the children and young people. Staff will hand on and be motivated to support the emotional development and well-being of children and young people if they feel that their own needs are being supported.

The National Healthy School Standard guidance on promoting staff health and well-being quotes Robert Rosen from The Healthy Company who says: 'Healthy people make health companies. And healthy companies are more likely, more often and over a longer period of time, to make healthy profits and to have healthy returns on their investments' (HDA, 2002: 6).

Support for staff health, well-being and emotional development must occur at two levels:

1 Support and opportunities to look after their own health and well-being, manage their stress levels and provide support for professional and personal issues which may be happening in and outside of work. This can happen in a range of ways, for example through:

   ■ Encouraging all staff to feel valued and participate in the decisions made across the school. (One of the many comments from school staff when we discuss children's participation is that they (school staff) would like the opportunity to participate in decision making)

   ■ Encouraging staff to appropriately discuss their feelings in relation to issues

   ■ Encouraging and facilitating a positive work–life balance

   ■ Provision of workplace counselling or peer support

   ■ Providing activities which increase morale such as negotiating cheaper access to the local sports facility or gym

   ■ Providing occasional 'treats' that will be valued by the staff and encouraging staff to enjoy activities or events as a team

2 Morris and Casey argue that 'emotionally literate schools show better learning outcomes for children, improved behavioural challenges and good relationships'. They argue that promoting emotionally literate staff through continuing professional development:

   ■ Helps to bring a supportive, warm and encouraging environment

   ■ Supports adults' ability to model emotionally literate ways of behaving

   ■ Develops staff ownership, confidence and competence in delivering the taught social and emotional curriculum (Morris and Casey, 2006: xvii–xviii)

Partnerships

There is a range of partnerships that, if effectively established and utilised, will help support your overall efforts to support the emotional and social development of children and young people.

The expert partner: children and young people

The United Nations (UN) Convention on the Rights of the Child sets out children and young people's rights to participate in decisions that affect them: 'Parties shall assure to the child, who is capable of forming his or own views, the right to express those freely in all matters affecting the child, the views of the child being given due weight in accordance with the age and maturity of the child' (United Nations, 1989).

The participation of children and young people has many benefits both for them and for professionals and communities working with them. This is a health-promoting opportunity in its own right. HeadsUpScotland (2005) is an organisation working to improve the mental health of children in Scotland. It identifies the following benefits of participation for children and young people.

- Being listened to improves their sense of well-being

- Opportunities for personal development, particularly among those who are often excluded

- Emotional well-being is developed through increased social networks and life choices

- Helps challenge negative stereotypes and images of mental and emotional health issues

- Empowers them to be creators of services not just consumers, and they are part of a process of positive change

- Enables sharing of experiences and learning together

These benefits are echoed by the children and young people involved in Young NCB[1] and were also identified through the *Getting It Together* project in Ireland run by the National Children's Bureau. Whilst participation activities often focus on a particular issue such as mental health, sexual health or drug awareness, the impact for children and young people of being involved in participatory processes where they have a voice, and their views and opinions are acted upon, is to promote a sense of emotional well-being, belonging and connectedness.

A young man involved in the Be Aware: Alcohol and Other Drugs (NCB with DEF, 2004) peer-led project who was disengaging from education reported feeling much more positive about himself and pleased with his contribution to the Be Aware project. Through the process he described 'realising he had something worthwhile to say'. This improved self-concept had in turn led to a greater commitment to his schooling, with his head teacher reporting improved attendance, effort and attainment which he attributed directly to the experience of participation.

---

[1] Young NCB is a free membership network that is part of the National Children's Bureau. They have an advisory group and, through a range of mechanisms, ensure the voices of children and young people are heard in internal and external policy- and decision-making.

Table 3.1   Principles of effective participation

1. Clear and visible commitment to involving children and young people with a route map of how to make it happen	• Every Child Matters and the Children Act (2004) require that children and young people are involved in decision making. All professionals working with children are expected to work towards enabling children and young people to develop the confidence and skills to make a positive contribution • The school works within the United Nations Convention for the Rights of the Child, fulfilling the child's right as set out in Article 12 to participate in all decisions that affect them • The way in which children and young people participate is clearly laid out in all policies • A governor and member of the school's SMT are identified as champion and monitor • The contribution of participation to emotional and social development, reducing bullying, developing key skills, raising attainment and raising achievement is recognised and understood
2. Children and young people's involvement is valued	• Children, families and the whole-school community recognise the importance of participation, the contribution it makes to education, inclusion and health targets and all work in partnership to develop a supportive culture and environment • Links to the taught curriculum (particularly PSHE and Citizenship and pastoral support) and other relevant process (such as personal education planning) are recorded and reported, and accreditation is sought where applicable, e.g. active citizenship programmes and Millennium Volunteers

3. Children and young people have equality of opportunity to be involved	• A wide range of activities is established and all children and young people are encouraged, supported and enabled to access participation opportunities
	   – these activities include identifying issues and areas of development as well as contributing to solutions
	   – they start where children and young people are at and often require explicit and creative targeting of those who may not normally volunteer or be nominated to participate
	   – extra support if offered where necessary for children and young people to access opportunities

4. Children and young people's participation and involvement are continually evaluated and reviewed	• Children and young people are given explicit feedback about how their views and ideas have been listened to, what action has been taken in response, and next steps. This is particularly important where decisions go against the wishes and ideas of children and young people • Adults, children and young people in school start at a level at which they feel confident and are able to build on by celebrating successes, valuing and learning from mistakes and maintaining creativity and motivation • Opportunities for reflection and evaluation are integral to the work
5. Quality standards	• Children, young people and staff receive training and support to develop their skills and confidence in organising, facilitating and participating in the full range of activities

Supporting parents and communities

Parents and carers play a huge role in promoting emotional health and well-being. Many need help and support to understand why it is so important to actively promote and take care of their child's emotional well-being at least as much as their physical well-being. It is helpful to involve parents and carers in their child's learning and the school's life through family learning and other means such as consultation events, working groups and open days.

Many schools offer clear practical advice for parents and carers about steps they can take to help improve their child's health and well-being and help reduce their stress levels within school. Any help and advice that is provided must be simple without being patronising, and with as little jargon as possible. Some parents, including those for whom English is not their first language and those who are not actively involved in their child's education, will need encouragement and support to engage with the school. This may be because they do not feel confident or trusting of the school for cultural reasons or because of their own poor experience of schooling. Some schools take the opportunity to include health displays and information at parents' evenings.

Case study: South Brent Primary School, Devon

In a Devon primary school (South Brent) staff identified a group of children about whom they had concerns. Their parents were invited to a one-to-one meeting with the ENABLE co-ordinator who, with their help and involvement, completed an ENABLE assessment of the child's emotional needs. This private meeting was conducted in a way that helped the parents to talk openly about the pressures in their lives and their concerns about their children. The openness of the discussion was facilitated by a simple explanation of how life circumstances affect a child's developments. The parents experienced themselves as being accepted, rather than judged or blamed, for their child's difficult behaviour. ENABLE action plans were drawn up, which included one-to-one work for the child with the co-ordinator, small-group work facilitated by the co-ordinator, teaching strategies for the class teacher and support staff, and simple strategies for the parents to use at home with the child.

After the initial success of this process, all staff were trained in the basic child development model that underpins ENABLE. With training and regular supervision, learning support staff are actively involved in interviewing parents and supporting children and their families. An evaluation of the project[2] (available from the school) revealed:

95 per cent thought ENABLE had a positive effect on their child at school

65 per cent had noticed improvements in the family since their child started ENABLE provision

82 per cent thought that ENABLE had helped their child to learn and achieve more

---

[2] Evaluation of the ENABLE Project at South Brent School (2005). Report available from Helen Nicholls, Head teacher, South Brent Primary School, Devon LA. Email: admin@south-brentprimary.devon.sch.uk.

Case study: Red Row County First School, Northumberland

Red Row County First School serves the communities of Red Row and Hadston in Central Northumberland. This is an area of social deprivation, and families are now experiencing third-generation unemployment following the closure of the coal mines. In the past two years the community has also lost many of its amenities, but is now an area of regeneration.

As a result of recent hardships the families have very low aspirations and self-esteem. Red Row has worked hard over the past few years to build relationships between the school and the parents/carers of our children. We have run a number of courses based around a variety of themes and these have been successful. However, we are aware that it is often the same people who attend these activities and we need to build upon our success with this in order to reach all of our families, not least the most vulnerable.

Red Row school is now piloting a new initiative, supported by an educational psychologist. This project will provide parents with a wide range of resources and services that will encourage parent participation; provide meaningful activities that engage the parents and encourage them to return week after week; and have a positive impact upon the lives of our students, their families and the community as a whole. In order to reach all parents we have developed a three-stage model that will use an existing mobile unit that is based on the school premises but not attached to the main building. The first stage of the model will be a Parent Information Point. This will provide a wide range of leaflets, guidance and support materials covering all aspects of health, housing and education. This can be accessed anonymously and will not need any intervention from other adults. This will be particularly attractive to those parents who have had negative experiences at school and feel too threatened to come into the main body of the school.

The second stage is a Universal Offer/entitlement of a range of workshops that have been designed as a result of consultation with parents and staff and will focus upon the key issues such as sleep, healthy eating, self-esteem, temper tantrums and language and other communication. These workshops will be practical and fun in order to engage parents, and will also involve sessions with their own children.

The third stage of the model will be more intense intervention with our most vulnerable families. On all the above stages we have sought funding and help through a range of specialist agencies including Psychological Services, Behaviour Support, the Child and Adult Mental Health Unit, school nurse and family support workers, who have now all committed to write and deliver the above sessions and provide literature and resources for the Parent Information Point. The project will benefit all our families in our school community.

The project will be monitored using the three main objectives as criteria:

1 Increasing numbers of parents using school resources and facilities
2 Increased commitment from parents
3 Improvement in attitudes and behaviour both within school and the outside community

(Continued)

(Continued)

We will use registers to monitor the numbers of parents, and questionnaires to evaluate the parents' perceptions and feelings. The local police officer will also be able to report on changes in behaviour within the community, alongside class teachers who will be able to measure the success of the project alongside reports from class teachers regarding the children's readiness for school. The project will be monitored on a half-termly basis and reports sent to all interested parties.

A parent involved in a family liaison project in the North East of England said that the most important thing they had learned through being involved with the school was the importance of playing with their child and taking an active interest in the things they are learning.

An independent day and boarding school in the South East of England provided the following advice for their parents through their monthly newsletter for parents:

- Try and talk to your child and ask them what is happening at school and in their lives. Be clear that you are not prying and you respect their space, but demonstrate you are interested. Even if they do not offer you much information find ways to continue to show you are interested
- Take time to come and watch them in assemblies, school plays, in sports events or concerts
- Tell them how important they are, look for the things that you like about them or you think they have done well, or areas they have made progress in and comment about it. Be specific and do it at a time when they will not be embarrassed. If you find it easier write them a note
- Reward them when they do well at least as often as you punish them when they do wrong
- If you are concerned about their behaviour changing, for example if they get withdrawn or stop doing things or change their friends and start doing different things, first ask them if they are OK and if there is anything happening they need help with. Name some of the things that you know may be happening, such as bullying, being over-stressed with school work or worried about changes in family life, and let them know they can talk if they want to. If you continue to be worried come and talk to their housemaster (but let them know you are thinking of contacting us first and give them a chance to talk to you)
- Make time to do things together that are fun together and help them get a balance of work and play. We expect a lot of our students and we work them hard, and they must get time to do things they enjoy and relax as well

The messages for adults, particularly parents and carers, set out in the box below were produced by secondary aged young people as part of the *Getting It Together* project.[3] They can be used as part of a meeting with parents and carers or reproduced (with acknowledgement of source) as part of a school newsletter. The leaflet is available to download from www.ncb.org.uk.

---

[3] Reproduced with thanks to Cooperation and Working Together, a mental health initiative working across the North and Republic of Ireland.

You can use a similar process to the one used here with the children in your school to create your own leaflet or newsletter. Simply ask children to either draw and write, discuss and record, or brainstorm as a whole class things they would like adults to know and understand so they can help children and young people through managing school, growing up, making career choices, studying and taking examinations or doing work experience. Parentline Plus provides a helpline and web-based resources to help and support parents (www.parentlineplus.org.uk).

Messages for adults

The *Getting It Together* team has been meeting over the past six months to think about young people's emotional health – what it means, why it is important and what helps promote good emotional health. We produced this leaflet for parents, carers and other adults because we think there are some things you can do to help us be brilliant and enjoy being young.

Feelings

Even though lots of things have changed since you were growing up if you think you still remember what it felt like to be young. How exciting it was, how scary it was and how sometimes you felt like no one would ever understand. None of that has changed – we still feel all those things and if you only remember how you felt, it will help you help us.

Talking

We need to keep talking about things, not just shouting and saying you are only young what do you know! We know what goes on when you are young and we could learn a lot from each other. If you keep saying, you are only young what do you know, we will just keep thinking, you are only old, what do you know!

Respect

For us to respect adults we need to be respected by them. We want to be believed and trusted and allowed to make mistakes. It is not fair that lots of adults treat us as though we are all silly and 'hoodies'. If you treat us like that, then that is probably how we are going to behave. If you respect us then of course we are going to respect you.

We are not children, but we are not adults either. We need your help!

Worries and concerns

Don't over worry but do stay concerned. Try and get the balance right. We know sometimes that is hard especially if we do something wrong, but we do appreciate the help that you give us, but that doesn't mean we can be perfect.

If we make mistakes and you are giving advice try to do it in such a way that it doesn't agitate or annoy us.

(Continued)

(Continued)

Mistakes

We are young, of course we will make lots of mistakes and we need a helping hand so we can learn from them. And even if you made that mistake as well I have to learn some things for myself anyway.

Encouragement

We need encouragement so we can have a go and try to do our best. It will be much easier to hear the criticisms and when we do things wrong if you tell us when we are doing things right as well.

Space

We need to do things on our own sometimes and have our own privacy. We don't want you to tell us everything about your life and even though you may want to know it doesn't mean you should know. Give us space and encouragement and we are more likely to talk to you about things anyway.

Help

Sometimes we need help from you and sometimes we will need to talk to a teacher or another professional. That doesn't mean anything bad to you, it just means it is easier for me to talk to someone else. Be pleased that I am talking to someone at all and respect my need for confidentiality.

Case study: Promoting communication between parents and children

Mentality is an organisation working to promote positive mental health. They have produced a resource 'Feeling good: promoting children's mental health'. The resource aims to promote dialogue between parents, carers and their children. It offers practical advice for parents on how to promote children's mental health including;

- Recognising the importance of parents valuing themselves and acknowledging their feelings
- Listening to children and offering them praise and respect
- Helping them develop self-control, setting clear limits and advice on managing difficult behaviours

The resource also provides a range of activity sheets to help discuss how they feel about different situations, exploring friendships, considering how others may feel and how they may respond to new situations and challenges. Through triggering discussions they can help children to develop emotional and social skills, and ensure that they are able to talk to parents and carers if they need help and support, for example, if they are being bullied or finding school work stressful.

For further information or to download the resource visit www.mentality.org.uk.

Partnerships with professionals working in and beyond schools

Schools are a central site for the 'joining up' of services at a local level. There are a range of partnerships with both statutory and non-statutory bodies that provide a range of help and advice to schools. Chapter 8 identifies the importance of one-to-one advice and support in schools and the community, and the significance of partnerships being developed to provide this one-to-one support. In addition agencies provide support to schools by:

- Providing expert advice and help on emotional health and well being including the research and best practice

- Offer training and support in different aspects of school strategies to promote emotional health and well-being including

  - Developing and using skills and tools for observing, recognising and responding to emotional needs and interruptions
  - Developing skills in planning and delivering Personal, Social and Health Education, peer support processes, managing massage in schools, leading stress reduction and anger management skills amongst children and young people

- Team teaching or providing support in delivery of strategies

- Providing small-group work for friendship groups or those identified as being at risk of exclusion

- Offering information about local trends and issues to inform localised strategies

- Provision of intensive support through Educational Psychology and Child and Adolescent Mental Health services for those children and young people who have acute needs

- Supporting and participating in funding bid development and implementation to try out new and innovative work with children and young people

- Providing new experiences and opportunities for managed risk and adventure in the community

Developing a supportive ethos and environment

Ethos

The ethos of a school is felt across all aspects of the school. It is the culture of the school – 'how things are done around here'. The development of a strong emotionally healthy ethos requires leadership from the Head, Governors and the Senior Leadership Team.

The ethos can be seen and felt in a number of ways including how staff look at and talk to each other and to the children in the school; whether there is any support for staff emotional health and well-being; whether senior staff doors are open or closed; the effort that is taken to reach out and participate in the wider community; whether people (staff, parents and carers and children) want to be there; how difference is valued and addressed; the type of and range of school furniture; access to toilets and drinking water; whether and what type of work is displayed, and how; whether and how children and young people play a role in decision-making and how that is managed; and the type and range of emotional, academic and extra-curricular support and opportunities there are available.

The ethos is not always completely tangible. Sometimes it simply feels like a nice place to be. Practitioners have identified the following as indicators of a positive ethos:

- The extent to which the whole-school staff and children demonstrate joy and engagement in learning and social interactions

- Whether the school makes active efforts to provide for the range of different learning, styles amongst children, including the use of the arts, drama and music

- Whether children, and young people enjoy coming to school and make the most of the opportunities and facilities offered

- The level of parental and community involvement in the school

- The range of partnerships, including the provision of specialist help and support

- Staff morale and how their welfare needs are attended to

- The stability of the workforce with a low rate of turnover and a range of ages, backgrounds and cultures represented in the staff group

- Levels of bullying and effective systems to address bullying

- Prompt mechanisms to support staff when they are in difficulty

- High rates of positive interactions between adults and children and children and children

- Demonstrable commitment to the welfare of children through strong pastoral systems and partnerships with external agencies

- The range and diversity of activities available

- The physical environment and how this reflects pride in the diverse school community and their achievements

Environment

The environment that children, young people and adults are 'working in' has a big impact on the way that they feel, how they think and the opportunities that are perceived to be available. It is the environment, which enables some of the core emotional needs to be met within a school.

If children and young people are coming into school tired as a result of their home circumstances, a school that provides sofas and quiet spaces for children to rest or snuggle up during lunchtime and breaks is likely to see a positive impact in behaviour and learning. One primary school found an increased interest in reading and improved literacy within a short time after introducing a number of sofas within the school. Children are often found snuggling up on the sofa resting comfortably in a safe space with a book.

Other core needs such as feeling and being safe are helpfully attended to within a school environment. For example, a school that displays prominently their commitment to ensuring that everyone feels safe sends a positive message to everyone, including visitors, that their welfare is cared for. Conversely, rooms that are dirty, too hot, too cold, damp or dreary will be difficult to be productive and excited in. Many schools display the work and achievements of their pupils around the school. Some schools now have artists in residence who help ensure the school is a bright, cheery and inspiring place to be.

KEY POINTS

- An effective policy framework underpins positive actions to promote emotional health and well-being

- There are a range of partners, including children and young people who are key partners in the development of strategy. The process of participating promotes emotional well-being

- The ethos and the physical environment need to be considered as part of the process of review and development

CHAPTER 4

Planning provision for promoting emotional and social development

This chapter explores the opportunities for promoting emotional development through curriculum and extra curricular activities. It provides advice and guidance, as well as case studies on:

■ Breakfast and after-school clubs

■ Assemblies

■ Personal, Social and Health Education

Planned activities that help children and young people develop emotional literacy and find strategies to support their own and the emotional health and well-being of others are a key part of the school's job in promoting emotional and social development.

Breakfast and after-school clubs

Through *Every Child Matters*, government pledged to ensure that all children have access to a range of activities beyond the school day. Breakfast clubs are increasingly commonplace across the UK and other parts of the world. They have been developed often in response to an increasing acknowledgement that a significant proportion of children and young people are coming to school without eating at all, or having eaten 'junk food' which hinders their health and well-being and their ability to learn.

A report by Ofsted (2006) concluded that schools that offer extended services including breakfast clubs, after-school clubs, holiday activities, health services and a range of therapies are helping to improve the self-confidence and achievement of children and young people in schools and their parents and carers. Some of the schools were already showing significant improvements in General Certificate of Secondary Education (GCSE) results. The report also said that pupils, particularly those who are disadvantaged, were gaining confidence in working with different agencies. This report, combined with the emerging evidence that eating breakfast has been associated with improved academic outcomes, improved concentration, increased school attendance and improved mood at school (Lucas and Liabo, 2004), demonstrates the importance of clubs and activities that are provided outside the school day.

There are a number of opportunities presented by breakfast and after-school clubs. These include:

- Building relationships with peers

- Building relationships with staff

- Promoting a sense of worth through involvement in the running of the club

- Developing new talents and skills

- Taking on different roles within groups and teams

- Being given and taking responsibility

Issues to consider in the development of breakfast and after-school clubs

1 What opportunities are there for children's participation and involvement in planning and running the clubs?

2 How will you encourage children, young people and families to participate in the activities and clubs?

3 Are the activities that are offered by the clubs diverse and responsive to the needs of the children, young people and their families?

4 If there are costs associated with attending clubs how will this impact on people's ability and willingness to participate?

5 How will you maximise the opportunities for building individual relationships with those who attend?

6 How will you make links with emotional development and health issues and provide support to access further information or support?

7 Will there be transport issues if attendance relies on getting to school early and leaving late, particularly if you are in a rural school or a special school where children and young people travel a long distance to school?

8 Which community organisations and individuals can help in the financing, running and profiling of the clubs and activities?

9 If individuals show real talent and/or interest, how will you nurture this and encourage them to develop their skills and talents further?

10 What are your indicators of success and how will you monitor and evaluate the activity?

Assemblies

School assemblies have the potential to be powerful opportunities to promote emotional well-being, to demonstrate the school is a caring community that values difference and diversity and the individual and group talents and achievements.

I remember my own school assemblies with a mixture of dread and bemusement as well as respect for the messages, and the powerful and passionate way they were sometimes conveyed. So powerful, that when I now meet 'random' people from my school days at conferences, seminars and events connected to emotional and social development, people who have long disappeared from my everyday conscious memory and have now become teachers, nurses and others involved in the care of children, we often recite the language of our assemblies that focused (not that we knew it then) on emotional resilience, such as *stickability* and *bounce-backability.*

The passion is what children and young people talk about, learn from, absorb and are inspired by, in assemblies and classrooms. They talk about the passion (or lack of it) and have often described the way an assembly is delivered as a film critic might describe an actor's performance.

Many children at primary level have talked about how the assemblies were great because they acknowledged their individual and group achievements. As many have also said, assembly reward-giving sometimes felt superficial or unenthusiastic – almost like a function that had to be endured. Some have also described how class assemblies or circle time is sometimes a more appropriate 'intimate' space for reflecting on achievements and offering rewards.

The National Primary Strategy in England has a package of materials to promote the Social and Emotional Aspects of Learning (SEAL). This package of materials includes assembly ideas (available from www.bandapilot.org.uk). A package of materials promoting Social, Emotional and Behavioural Skills (SEBS) is currently being piloted for secondary schools. These materials will be available from September 2007.

In planning the assembly and its active delivery consider:

- How will you ensure the content and delivery is relevant to the particular group?

- How will children and young people know you feel enthusiastic and passionate about the issue?

- What preparation and follow-up is needed in the classroom?

- How will you ensure that individuals know how to access confidential, one-to-one support if the assembly has raised particular issues for them?

Personal, Social and Health Education

Personal, Social and Health Education is the planned provision for promoting emotional and social development in schools. It includes three elements:

- The acquisition of accessible information that is relevant to children and young people's lives and experiences, maturity and understanding

- Exploration, clarification and development of attitudes and values that support self-esteem and are positive to health and well-being

- Development of personal and social skills to enable emotional development and interaction with others as well as making positive health choices and actively participating in society

Personal, Social and Health Education enables children and young people to develop the motivation, autonomy, knowledge and skills to ensure they stay safe, keep healthy, enjoy and achieve, make a positive contribution and enjoy economic and social well-being. It includes a range of themes and issues which impact on emotional health and well-being, such as:

- Prejudice and discrimination

- Relationships ✷

- Rights and responsibilities

- Stereotypes and expectations

- Bullying and violence

- Emotional literacy and the management of feelings

- Stress and anger management

- The links between emotional health and well-being and risk taking behaviours

- Transition and change (including the physical and emotional changes during puberty and adolescence)

- Loss, separation and grief

- Access to help services

- Self and sexual identify

Personal, Social and Health Education also provides opportunities to consider emotional issues and develop emotional and social skills which support children and young people's ability to ✷ actively participate in their school and communities, as well as make choices, develop life skills such as decision-making and assertiveness, and to look after their health and well-being.

To be effective the evidence from research and practice suggests PSHE must:

- Be delivered in the context of positive relationships between the facilitator and peers ✷

- Be supported by a whole-school commitment and ethos   *NGs aim to do this*

- Start early and be developmentally appropriate *– links to early intervention*

- Include acquisition of information, development of skills, and exploration of emotions, feelings, attitudes and values

- Be delivered within a safe, supportive learning environment with people working *as a group* (not simply in a group)

- Use active learning methods which meet different learning styles

- Ensure effective differentiation so it is challenging and interesting for all

- Develop a critical awareness of messages in the media

- Develop and reinforce positive values and messages including respect and equality

- Is relevant to their own lives and, through effective assessment for learning, opportunities for behaviour change are encouraged

- Well linked to confidential advice and support services including helplines

- Is both mainstream – an entitlement for all – and targeted to meet the needs of the most vulnerable

The SEBS and SEAL materials produced as part of the National Strategies for raising achievement in English primary and secondary schools are excellent as part of a planned programme of Personal, Social and Health Education. They are available from www.bandapilot.org.uk and www.standards.dfes.gov.uk.

There are a number of resources, materials and approaches that are helpful in planning and delivering PSHE. The National Children's Bureau has produced an overview, introductory document, 'A whole school approach to PSHE and Citizenship', which sets out best practice principles. It is available, alongside a range of briefings and different aspects of PSHE, free at www.ncb.org.uk.

The PSHE Subject Association also provides advice and guidance on developing and implementing effective PSHE practice, at www.pshe-association.org.uk.

Below are two case studies of materials and approaches that have proven helpful.

Case study: *Cards for Life*

Cards for Life is an innovative pack for working with young people aged 11 upwards. It is a pack of 40 scenario-based cards which is divided into five categories as set out in the Children Act (2004):

- Being healthy
- Staying safe
- Enjoying and achieving
- Making a positive contribution
- Economic well-being

Based on the Respect Research and developed with the active involvement of young people, the scenarios are based on real-life issues and dilemmas that are relevant to young people.

(Continued)

They cover issues such as decision-making, peer influence, risk-taking, alcohol and other drugs, bullying, sexual health, citizenship, friendships. (Blank cards are also included so workers can develop their own scenarios which are relevant to the particular context they are working in.)

On the back of each card is a standard set of questions (see following page) encouraging young people (either individually or in groups) to think about the scenario and identify what is happening for the different people that are involved. It then encourages them to think about the thoughts, feelings and possible actions and consider their own feelings and what they have learnt from the experience of undertaking the activity. It is the combination of considering the experiences of others, the exploration of actions and the reflection on their own feelings and how they would apply the learning to real life that has proven helpful in using the cards with young people.

The pack can be used in group and one-to-one situations, they can be used to trigger discussion and inform the development of arts based or research activities. Further information about *Cards for Life* is available from www.ncb.org.uk

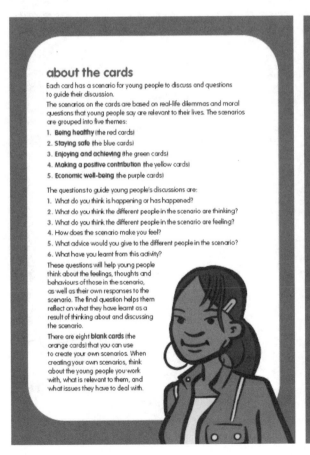

about the cards

Each card has a scenario for young people to discuss and questions to guide their discussion.

The scenarios on the cards are based on real-life dilemmas and moral questions that young people say are relevant to their lives. The scenarios are grouped into five themes:

1. **Being healthy** (the red cards)
2. **Staying safe** (the blue cards)
3. **Enjoying and achieving** (the green cards)
4. **Making a positive contribution** (the yellow cards)
5. **Economic well-being** (the purple cards)

The questions to guide young people's discussions are:

1. What do you think is happening or has happened?
2. What do you think the different people in the scenario are thinking?
3. What do you think the different people in the scenario are feeling?
4. How does the scenario make you feel?
5. What advice would you give to the different people in the scenario?
6. What have you learnt from this activity?

These questions will help young people think about the feelings, thoughts and behaviours of those in the scenario, as well as their own responses to the scenario. The final question helps them reflect on what they have learnt as a result of thinking about and discussing the scenario.

There are eight **blank cards** (the orange cards) that you can use to create your own scenarios. When creating your own scenarios, think about the young people you work with, what is relevant to them, and what issues they have to deal with.

The red cards focus on being healthy:

talking about contraception and safer sex ● changing bodies ● using solvents ● drugs and parents ● personal hygiene ● drugs and peer pressure ● staying in control ● pregnancy and abortion

The blue cards focus on staying safe:

getting help ● effects of alcohol ● helping others stay safe ● pornography ● sexual identity and trust ● mental illness and bullying ● standing up for yourself ● overcoming personal fears

The green cards focus on enjoying and achieving:

making choices when under pressure ● parents' expectations ● balancing work and play ● not fitting in ● hopes and fears about the future ● feeling valued ● being yourself ● hobbies

The yellow cards focus on making a positive contribution:

envy and jealousy ● pride in the community ● stealing ● taking part in protests ● helping people ● impact of prejudice ● damaging the efforts of others ● tolerance and support

The purple cards focus on economic well-being:

managing on a budget ● racism ● stealing and friendship ● choosing between parents ● being a teenage parent ● achieving at school ● saving for the future ● donating to charity

The orange cards have been left blank for you to develop your own scenarios.

Figure 4.1   Cards for Life

making choices when under pressure

Jasmine has got exams coming up. She is dreading them because, however hard she tries, she just can't remember all the things she thinks she needs to know. Someone offers Jasmine a pill that they say will help her to stay alert.

sexual identity and trust

Gary is gay. He plucks up the courage to tell James, his best friend. After this, people start to whisper and crack gay jokes when Gary is around. Gary is sure James has told people, but James denies it. They have been best friends since primary school and Gary wants to believe James.

talking about contraception and safer sex

Lee is going out with Kerry and feels ready to have sex. Lee is too embarrassed to talk about using condoms. Nobody else seems to bother about pregnancy and HIV anyway, and he thinks it will spoil the fun.

things to talk about

1 What do you think is happening or has happened?
2 What do you think the different people in the scenario are thinking?
3 What do you think the different people in the scenario are feeling?
4 How does the scenario make you feel?
5 What advice would you give to the different people in the scenario?
6 What have you learnt from this activity?

Figure 4.2   Cards for Life

Case study: *Getting It Together cards*

Getting It Together is a pack of cards for working with young people on emotional health and was developed as part of the Irish youth-led project funded by Cooperation and Working Together. The cards focus on different issues relating to young people and emotional well-being. They are designed to stimulate discussion in group and one-to-one settings. They are divided into five sections: True or False? Why? What and How? Describe a Time and The Feel Good Factor.

The cards have been developed in collaboration with young people. They adopt a very broad and grounded approach to emotional health and well-being, encouraging young people to think about, for example, the links between prejudice and emotional health; how emotional health affects school or college work; how sleep and physical activity are related to emotional health and well-being; the importance of friendships and where and how to access help and support.

One at a time, young people are encouraged to take a card, read it out and then provide their own response before the facilitator opens up the issue for wider discussion. Supporting notes are included. Further information about *Getting It Together* is available at www.ncb.org.uk.

Cross-curricular approaches

Many other curriculum areas, including English and Science, provide opportunities for promoting emotional development through both the process of learning and the opportunities for discussing and exploring related issues such as prejudice and discrimination. In 2003, the Gulbenkian Foundation published a report, *Improving Science and Emotional Development*, based on a study of the role of science in promoting social and emotional skills and the role of emotional skills and collaborative approaches in improving science. Through the project the author concluded that the use of collaborative learning techniques enables:

- Pupils to learn to get on with each other and support each other's learning

- Pupils to develop socially and understand each other more

- Confidence to develop about working collaboratively with members of the same and the opposite sex

- An increase in their scientific understanding as they learn to work together in groups (Matthews, B., 2003)

As young people involved in the project said:

It's [Science] made a lot easier because you mix with different people that you wouldn't normally mix with before, so you get to know them more.
It's better to learn in groups because you learn more when you work with other people.

59

This is supported by Cohen (1994) who states, 'when groups engage in cooperative tasks, they are more likely to form friendly ties, to trust each other and to influence each other ... (research) shows those who (come) from classes using cooperative learning methods show far more helpful and cooperative behaviour'.

KEY POINTS

- Provision for emotional and social development is best ensured across the curriculum and extra-curricular activities. Personal, Social and Health Education is an important vehicle for promoting emotional and social development

- Breakfast clubs and after-school activities provide real opportunities to strengthen relationships between peers and staff and pupils

- The process of learning in all lessons is at least important as what is taught about emotional health and well-being

Campaigns and awareness-raising events

There are a number of issues relevant to emotional health and well-being that are the focus of specific national campaigns and awareness-raising events. There are also locally organised campaigns. This chapter provides a broad overview of some relevant campaigns. Given the impact of bullying on children and young people, it then provides an in-depth focus and case study on anti-bullying policy and practice, including details of an anti-bullying week which takes place in England.

National campaigns and awareness-raising events

There are a number of nationally led campaigns, events and awareness-raising days that address and relate to emotional health and well-being, such as Mental Health Day and Anti-Bullying Week. These provide a useful focus for activities within school for a number of reasons, including:

- There are often *nationally produced packages of information and support* that are made available in hard copy and on line

- *Competitions* are sometimes organised nationally and regionally which encourage and motivate children to join in and think about an issue

- Local agencies with an interest and expertise organise *local community events* which can enable capacity-building/training opportunities for school staff, and awareness-raising within families and communities

- Local agencies have the *capacity and capability to offer particular support* and work with schools to raise the profile of the issues

- *Funding* is often available for small projects

- There is often a *media profile* which reinforces and supports work in school or can be a stimulus for lesson and assembly ideas

- Celebrities are often involved which can provide the 'cool factor' and encourage children and young people to hear the message. In addition local celebrities may be encouraged to participate in community activities

- Local businesses or associations, for example the Rotary Club, may provide resourcing and support for events

Relevant awareness-raising days in England and other parts of the UK and, how to find out more about them, include:

- Mental Health Day on 10 October each year, which is organised by the World Federation for Mental Health (WfMH) who produce a pack to support activities. Further information is available at www.wfmh.org

- *Anti-Bullying Week* in November each year and which has a dedicated theme. Further information is available from the Anti-Bullying Alliance www.antibullying alliance.org.uk

- Play Day often with a theme, which focuses on the emotional health benefits of playing. Play Day is in August each year. Further information is available from Play England at www.playengland.org.uk

- World AIDS Day on 1 December each year, often having a theme, which focuses on prejudice, stigma and discrimination. It is a global event organised by UNAIDS. In England it is coordinated by the National AIDS Trust www.nat.org.uk

- Disability awareness, an independent-living exhibition and a family fun day rolled into one. The main aim of the day is to promote independence throughout life and work. For further information www.disabilityawarenessday.co.uk

- Lesbian, gay, bisexual and transgender (LGBT) history month – LGBT History Month (February) aims to mark and celebrate the lives and achievements of lesbian, gay, bisexual and trans people. Further information is available at www.lgbthistory-month.org.uk

- Black History Month, which has been celebrated across the UK every October for over 30 years. It is a time when we highlight and celebrate the achievements of the black community and uncover hidden history about our communities. For further information go to www.blackhistorymonthuk.co.uk

Case study: It's prejudice that's queer

The Terence Higgins Trust developed a campaign focusing on the impact of prejudice and stigma on people's well-being and, consequently, their relationships and sexual health. It's prejudice that's queer used a range of media including billboards and advertorials in magazines and newspapers. A school in South London used the campaign as an opportunity to raise awareness of homophobia and the negative impact of it on the school and the school community. A range of activities took place including:

■ an assembly led by the head teacher confirming their commitment to support all students and to taking homophobia seriously. This was followed by sixth form drama students performing a piece they had written about homophobia

■ focused PSHE lessons addressing prejudice and discrimination, and specifically homophobia. These lessons went across the year groups and were planned according to their age and maturity. Older year groups used the campaign materials as the basis for discussion.

■ information about local youth groups, services and national helplines, as well as in-school help and advice was provided and posted on noticeboards

Anti-bullying

All the evidence shows that bullying has an impact on the emotional and social development of children and young people, and on their emotional health and well-being.

The Anti-Bullying Alliance (www.antibullyingalliance.org) defines bullying as:

A subjective experience that can take many forms. Accounts of children and young people, backed up by research, identify bullying as any behaviour that is:

■ *harmful, carried out by an individual or a group*
■ *repetitive, wilful or persistent*
■ *an imbalance of power, leaving the person being bullied feeling defenceless.*

Bullying generally fits into one of two categories: emotionally or physically harmful behaviour. It can include any of the following: name-calling, taunting, threats, mocking, making offensive comments, kicking, hitting, pushing, taking and damaging belongings, gossiping, excluding people from groups, and spreading hurtful and untruthful rumours. These actions can take place face to face, via third parties, or via other means such as text messages and emails.

Children, young people and adults can instigate bullying and be bullied in schools. The nature of bullying is changing and evolving as technology develops. What is clear is that bullying has a destructive and harmful effect on children and young people's lives, not just in relation to the person who is being bullied, but also to those who bully and those who stand by. It can lead to self-doubt, lack of confidence, low self-esteem, depression, anxiety and self-harm, and sometimes even suicide.

In recent years there has been a greater than ever before focus worldwide on reducing bullying and the harm it causes. It is now widely acknowledged that bullying is 'not just another fact of life' and is not a normal part of childhood that helps build character. The Anti-Bullying Alliance provides a range of materials that set out the research, evidence and best practice information in regards to anti-bullying. Further information can be found from their website: www.anti-bullyingalliance.org.uk.

Evidence from research and practice has shown that often the same children and young people are being bullied as are doing the bullying and sometimes being bystanders too. Often those who are emotionally damaged or have been hurt or abused by adults will redirect that hurt at others in a range of ways, including bullying.

There is no simple dichotomy between the 'bully' and the 'victim'. Adopting approaches which recognise the complexity of bullying and move beyond this simplistic characterisation of how bullying happens is important.

An effective anti bullying strategy involves three elements:

Prevention

- Preventing bullying through a whole-school approach; focusing on creating a culture where bullying is unacceptable. This is done through the range of strategies outlined in this book, including behaviour policies assemblies, Personal, Social and Health Education, Citizenship and active participation such as school councils and survey work such as what types of bullying happens and where does it take place? This is supported by effective pastoral systems, including peer support.

Reacting and responding to bullying incidents

- Responding effectively to bullying using reward and sanctions as outlined in your behaviour policy. The key tasks in responding effectively are:
  - Making sure the person being bullied is safe and feels safe
  - Establishing what happened by listening to different perspectives, including those of the person bullied, the person doing the bullying and those that have been 'bystanders'[1]
  - Making sure the person who is doing the bullying knows it is wrong to bully, takes responsibility for their behaviour and makes amends. Doing this in an emotionally intelligent way will require focusing on the unacceptable behaviours being displayed, and not reinforcing a sense of the individual being bad
  - Publicly signalling, where necessary and appropriate, to the whole school that the bullying is taken seriously and has been responded to well. This will often including talking to and with parents and carers

Providing longer-term support to those bullying and those being bullied

- Identifying immediate and longer-term support needs of both the person being bullied and the person who has done the bullying. This may include friendship-based group work, accessing support from external agencies including voluntary agencies and Child Adolescent Mental Health Services

  - Recording the bullying incident including what happened and who was involved, including the bystanders

---

[1] A bystander is a person who has witnessed the bullying. See Ball (2006).

- Reflecting on the process to identify any lessons for the future and disseminating any learning to colleagues
- Monitoring and following up with all parties concerned to ensure that the bullying has stopped and, if it has not, taking appropriate steps

Figure 5.1   Example of an anti-bullying postcard

Anti-Bullying Week

In some countries there is a national Anti-Bullying Week which provides a focused opportunity to raise awareness of schools' commitment to preventing bullying, dealing with it effectively when it does happen, and promoting emotionally and physically safe school communities. In England Anti-Bullying Week is organised by the Anti-Bullying Alliance, comprising of over 60 organisations who work together. Each year a theme is agreed which profiles a particular aspect of bullying considered to be of importance.

For further information about anti-bullying (and Anti-Bullying Week in England) visit the Anti-Bullying Alliance website at www.anti-bullyingalliance.org.uk or, for international perspectives, visit www.stopbullyingworld.com.

Case study: Anti-Bullying Week 2006

Anti-Bullying Week in England is the third week of November. The theme for 2006 was the role of the bystander, with the campaign theme 'Bullying: See It. Get Help. Stop it.' Nationally the Anti-Bullying Alliance (ARA) role is to provide background materials and stimulate regional and local activities within school and the community for Anti-Bullying Week. Following the idea of a young man in the North East, the last Friday of Anti-Bullying Week is nominated as Blue Friday – a non-uniform day – where children and young people are encouraged to wear blue to show their solidarity against bullying.

Limited edition anti-bullying lanyards were produced which schools and community settings were able to buy in packs of 50. In turn children and young people paid to participate in the non-uniform day and received a lanyard. Additional funds from the lanyard raised were used in a variety of ways, including allocation to the School Council to spend on anti-bullying work or given to local and national charities.

A series of postcards with different messages was also produced (see previous page). These have space on the back for children and young people to fill in details of bullying in their school or community or give their ideas for stopping bullying, and either place them in an 'anti- bullying box' or hand them to a teacher, social worker, youth worker or parent or carer.

Trutex (the school uniform provider) was the official sponsor of Anti-Bullying Week and worked with the Anti-Bullying Alliance to run a national poster competition. Judges included Trutex, ABA and children and young people. Three designs were chosen and produced as the official poster. It was also supported by the Department for Education and Skills and Hope Education. Nickelodeon was the official broadcaster, and ran a parallel campaign 'See something Say something', Nickelodeon UK's campaign to unite and empower children to speak out against bullying. Working alongside the Anti-Bullying Alliance as the official broadcaster for Anti-Bullying Week 2006, the Nickelodeon initiative was the biggest ever undertaken by a UK broadcaster, encompassing television, the web and schools. You can find out more information about the UK's biggest ever anti-bullying television initiative at nick.co.uk/saysomething.

Further information about Anti-Bullying Week is available at www.antibullyingalliance.org.uk.

KEY POINTS

- ■ Campaigns provide a useful focus for promoting emotional health and well-being
- ■ Free materials and training are often available for schools to utilise
- ■ Bullying is a serious issue which needs addressing within schools

CHAPTER 6

Promoting calmness, anger management and stress reduction

This chapter sets out a range of tried and tested approaches to promoting calmness, conflict resolution, anger management and stress reduction. As massage is one of these techniques, it also includes an example of safe touch policy.

We also need to promote the emotional state, such as calmness, a sense of well-being, and feeling safe and valued, that make it easier to learn. If learners arrive in, or get into, a stressed state it is well worth taking the time to de-stress them through relaxation techniques or a physical activity. (Weare, 2004: 5)

Circle time

Circle time is a proactive creative approach, which is used to promote positive relationships and behaviour within the school. To be effective, circle time is used in an ongoing way, with children and the adults who work with them coming together and sitting in a circle to discuss feelings, thoughts and issues that are affecting the day-to-day life of the school. Circle time has been demonstrated to reduce bullying, aid conflict resolution and improve emotional literacy. Through circle time, children learn about negotiation, listening to each other, expressing a view and listening to the views of others.

Further information about circle time is available at www.teachernet.gov.uk. (See also Useful resources and organisations.)

Improving co-ordination and concentration

Many schools use exercise to improve co-ordination and promote learning, through physical movement to develop concentration and memory, co-ordination and a readiness to learn. Those who use these on a regular basis have seen a dramatic improvement in learning and behaviour as a result. Michelle Draisey, a special educational needs support teacher and life coach specialising in working with children, has developed a programme of activities which are used regularly with classes of children across the primary school. This has had a significantly positive impact on children's confidence, self-esteem and therefore ability to learn. To find out about the activities programme, contact Two Plus Consultants at www.twoplus.net.

There are other websites and support materials available for this area of work including www.braingym.org.

Visualisation

Visualisation similarly offers children and young people a space and a place that relaxes them and makes them feel positive or helps them to learn and develop empathy through imagination and visualisation. It can also, when facilitated well, enable them to imagine themselves achieving new things, exploring new ideas and in this way can promote confidence and a willingness to try.

Figure 6.1   Visualisation images on sense CD

Making Sense of Growing Up and Keeping Safe, a CD-ROM for Key Stage 2 addresses the five national outcomes for children as set out in the Children Act (2004). It provides specific activities on emotional well-being including a scene of the characters participating in a visualisation as a way of relaxing at the end of the school day. The visualisation is based on a real activity carried out in a primary school in Essex. Guidance on carrying out the visualisation and ideas for follow-up activities about emotional health and well-being are provided in the supporting notes.

Further information is available at www.sensecds.com.

Safe spaces

Many schools create safe areas within either the classroom or school so when children and young people get angry or stressed they are able to 'self-refer' or are given opportunities to take time out. Having squeezy balls, a range of fabrics or other items to touch can help children manage and regain charge of feelings and behaviours.

Massage in Schools

Massage in schools is a positive behaviour strategy. It is a relatively recent development in schools and is based on the idea that children attending school experience structured positive and nurturing touch from other children. No child touches another without consent. The children are taught a simple sequence of movements linked to stories. They learn how to give and receive safe touch on the back and arms. Research (Sutherland, 2005) shows that this has a very positive impact on children's relationships with each other, reducing behaviour incidents and name-calling, and increasing children's acceptance of diversity. The session is led at first by a trained teacher/facilitator. In schools where the programme has run for a while, sessions are sometimes led by class members, supervised by the teacher.

Safe touch is important developmentally for all children. Children first learn how to contain their feelings by the ways in which their primary carer helps them to regulate, for example by soothing their distress or joining them in their excitement. By the time children come into schools, their brains will already have rudimentary stress management systems based on these experiences. Most children will have experienced safe and helpful touch but a minority may have experienced touch as invasive or harmful. In order for schools to make safe touch available in appropriate ways, a 'Safe Touch Policy' is required establishing clear boundaries. Once developed it needs an effective implementation plan, including training.

Case study: Massage in schools

VT a head teacher with 12 years' experience in a primary school in a deprived area of London agreed to a meeting with a Massage in Schools Programme Instructor. During the meeting the instructor informed VT of the many benefits of the daily child-to-child massage programme performed over school uniform on the backs, head, neck, shoulders and arms. The benefits to her children, her staff and her school were discussed.

VT was particularly impressed by how the programme encouraged a safe, relaxed environment that supported learning and positive friendships, leading to reduced bullying. VT agreed to introduce the programme into one Year 3 class for one term and monitor the incidents of fracas both within the classroom and in the playground. She also monitored the change in behaviour of one child (with the parent's permission) and recorded the views of the teacher.

The programme was introduced by the Massage in Schools Programme instructor over three weeks. At first children found working in directed pairs difficult but soon began to voice how they loved the massage and enjoyed the daily routine. Children said they were happy with more friends.

The benefits to the teacher were soon obvious, as children were quieter, calmer and concentrating for longer periods. Other learning skills, such as co-operation and confidence increased. Children's increased self-esteem was noted through increased positive interaction with the teacher and peers.

(Continued)

(Continued)

The teacher found, over the term, that the child with identified learning difficulties, showed a decrease in disruptive behaviour in both the classroom and the playground. He began to be accepted within the group setting. His concentration had improved with an increase of almost 50 per cent longer on task and his handwriting skills had improved. He also co-operated with the teacher and peers on his table.

VT noted that no child's name from the massage class was in the playground incident log since the start of the Massage Programme. It was because of this one undisputed fact that VT agreed for the Massage in Schools Programme to be rolled out throughout the entire school.

It is absolutely vital that schools, and those who work with them, work within an agreed policy framework and are trained and understand why touch is helpful, how to touch children and young people safely and appropriately, and establish clear, consistent boundaries. This is essential, so that everyone knows what the rules are and how to follow them. The example policy below demonstrates how one school has approached, safe touch. (See Appendix 1 for the full version of the Safe Touch Policy.)

Example Safe Touch Policy[1]

Introduction

Children learn who they are and how the world is in relationship. The quality of the child's relationships with significant adults is key to their healthy development and emotional health and wellbeing.

Research

Research shows clearly that healthy pro-social brain development requires access to safe touch as one of the means of calming, soothing and containing distress for a frightened, sad or angry child. It is essential for all children to learn the difference between safe and unsafe touch and to experience having their strongest emotions contained, validated, accepted and soothed by a significant adult. If children are behaving in unacceptable, threatening, dangerous, aggressive or out-of-control ways, they have not yet learned how their strongest emotional reactions can be contained, channelled and communicated safely. In recognition of this, *under special, agreed and supervised conditions*, specially trained staff will consider using

---

[1] This guidance and draft policy was first developed by Lynne Gerlach within the context of a specialist ENABLE project in a Primary School. Other schools wishing to adapt the policy would need to adapt it to fit their particular circumstances. The copyright of this policy is restricted to Sowelu Associates 2005.

2 Safe touch is seen as problematic, which is why this book is looking at a particular case study and examining how that worked. It is advocating 'safe touch' only in the context of appropriate training and procedures.

(Continued)

safe touch as one of the means available to them for example to calm a distressed child, contain an angry or wild child and/or encourage or affirm an anxious child or a child with low self-esteem. Safe touch used to calm, soothe and regulate a child's emotions is a needed developmental experience. The brain does not develop self-soothing neuronal pathways unless and until this safe emotional regulation has been experienced. Where children have had insufficient experience of safe touch and calming regulation this may be a priority to help the brain to develop access to thinking, judging and evaluating mechanisms. Safe touch is one of the key ways of regulating children's emotions but it is a strategy that *fully trained*

staff will use only under supervision and in line with a whole-school Policy on Touch. Other means of calming, soothing and containing children's strong emotions include:

- Slowing one's pace

- Lowering the voice

- Breathing more deeply

- Initially matching the pitch and volume of the child's emotional display (shout, cry, and so on) and then regulating it down

- Talking slowly firmly and quietly in an unhurried unflustered way

Context

Our policy on touch has been developed in the context of the local education authority (LEA) Child Protection Procedures and Policies. It takes into account the extensive neurobiological research and other empirical studies relating to attachment theory and child development that identify safe touch as a positive contribution to brain development, emotional regulation, mental health and the development of pro-social skills.

Who does the policy apply to?

All staff and children working within the specialist project/or pastoral team.

Identified staff are trained by a specialist child psychotherapist/education inspector in the identification and use of safe touch as a developmental intervention. All of the staff team receive regular case supervision with a specialist consultant and their day-to-day practice is monitored by the project co-ordinator and the head teacher.

Why have a policy on touch?

In order to protect children and school staff from allegations under Child Protection procedures most schools and LEAs have adopted 'No Touch' policies. However this school is

(Continued)

(Continued)

adopting an informed, evidence-based decision to allow safe touch in special cases as a developmentally appropriate intervention that will aid healthy growth and learning.[2]

Safe touch is one of the key ways of regulating children's emotions but it is a strategy that fully trained staff will use *only* under supervision and in line with the school's Policy on Touch.

The developmentally appropriate (and therapeutic) use of safe touch is defined by situations in which abstinence would actually be inhumane, unkind and potentially psychologically or neurobiologically damaging. Examples include the empirically backed beneficial use of touch in the comforting of a child who is an acute state of distress and/or out of control. Not to reach out to the child in such circumstances could be re-traumatising and neurobiologically damaging, confirming or inviting anti-social behaviour patterns. Abstinence in the face of intense grief, stress and/rage reactions can lead to a state of hyperarousal, in which toxic levels of stress chemicals are released in the body and brain. The severely damaging long-term effects of this state have been intensively researched worldwide and are well documented.

Moreover, gentle safe holding is appropriate if a child is:

- Hurting himself/herself or others (or is likely to hurt himself/herself and/or others) or

- Damaging property, and/or

- Incensed and out of control, so that all verbal attempts to engage him/her have failed.

Such necessary interventions are fully in line with guidelines set out in the government document, *New Guidance on the Use of Reasonable Force in School* (DfEE, 1998).

The staff team members are thoroughly trained in the safest and gentlest means of holding a child which is entirely designed to enable the child to feel safe and soothed, and to bring him or her down from uncontrollable states of hyperarousal. Whilst limits and boundaries in such circumstances can be a vital corrective emotional experience, without such an intervention (holding) the child can be left at risk of actual physical or psychological damage.

Appropriate and inappropriate touch

We are highly aware of the current atmosphere where, owing to fears of abuse, touch as a natural and important form of human connection has been almost vetoed in some school

---

[2] Touch is sometimes seen as problematic, which is why this book is looking at a particular case study and examining how that worked. It is advocating 'safe touch' only in the context of appropriate training and procedures.

(Continued)

contexts. Our policy rests on the belief that *every* member of staff needs to appreciate the difference between appropriate and inappropriate touch. Hence all staff have to demonstrate a clear understanding of the difference. They have to show themselves to be highly aware of both the damaging and unnecessary uses of touch in an educational context. Touch is not to be used as an ill thought out or impulsive act of futile reassurance/gratification or as a block to referral for psychological assessment.

Equally, when a child is in deep distress, the ENABLE team member is trained to know when and how sufficient connection and psychological holding have been or can be provided/established *without* touching.

Safe touch guidelines

To ensure touch is only used appropriately the following guidelines are followed:

■ *Parents/carers* are informed of the school policy around Touch

■ *Parents/carers* provide signed consent for their child to be part of the ENABLE program

■ *Parents/carers* wherever possible are involved in the ENABLE Assessments and Action Plans and are regularly updated as to their child's progress through the program

■ *Teachers and support staff* are trained in the ENABLE approach

■ *Teachers and support staff* are trained in all aspects of safe touch

■ *Staff members* should agree the use of safe touch in discussion with their case supervisor *and its use recorded and monitored (optional)*

■ *2 adult rule:* no adult should use touch when alone with a child

■ *Use* brief, gentle contact on open clothed parts of the body: hands, arms, shoulders, head, hair, shoes

Unsafe touch

■ *At no point and under no circumstances* should staff members use touch to satisfy their own need for physical contact or reassurance

■ *No unsafe touch:* all staff are trained to be fully cognisant of touch that is invasive or which could be confusing, traumatising or experienced as eroticising in any way whatsoever. If any such touch is used it is deemed as the most serious breach of the Code of Ethics warranting the highest level of disciplinary action.

KEY POINTS

■ There is a range of approaches and techniques that children and young people can be taught to promote calmness and reduce stress

■ Integrating these techniques into the everyday life of school can help children and young people integrate them into their lives

■ Safe touch is an important experience for children. Schools need to plan carefully and ensure they have a clear policy before establishing any work that involves touch

HAPTER 7

Play and creativity

This chapter sets out the importance of play and creativity in promoting emotional and social development. It explores the importance of providing new opportunities to stretch children's horizons. It also offers a detailed practical case study of the work of an artist in residence in a primary school, and practical activities for promoting emotional literacy.

Play and creativity are key in helping children develop friendship and interpersonal skills, and it allows us to learn about cause and effect, to develop risk assessment and management skills, to seek and get thrills and experience adrenaline, to develop motor neurone co-ordination skills and a sense of their body's abilities. It also helps them to learn to share and compromise, to develop an awareness of the impact of their behaviour on others, to get on with people different from them and to learn different roles. Play is a real way of developing the brain – for example, safe rough and tumble and playing on bouncy castles help brain growth and the connectivity and development which helps promote emotional well-being. Having opportunities for play and creativity is every child's entitlement and right. The UN Convention on the Rights of the Child recognises children's rights 'to rest and leisure, to engage in play and recreational activities appropriate to the age of the child and to participate freely in cultural life and the arts' (United Nations, 1989: Article 31).

The different types of play sit along a spectrum, from free play through to play therapy. In *Getting Serious about Play*, free play is defined as 'what children do when they follow their own ideas and interests, in their own way and for their own reasons' (DCMS, 2004). Further along the spectrum is organised and structured play, where children are encouraged to learn new skills or to understand different concepts and ideas. Further along still, are activities that may help to improve motor neurone coordination. Finally comes play therapy, which is perhaps most famously explored through books such as *Dibs: In Search of Self* (Axline, 1966).

Creativity, too, is a broad term that spans the full range of the arts, such as physical dance and theatre, drama, sculpture, textiles and drawing. In *All our Futures* (QCA, 2000) creativity is defined as multidimensional, which involves 'using imagination, pursuing purposes, being original and judging value'. It goes on to emphasise that creative energies and expression can be nurtured and developed in everyone.

Research and evidence from practice shows that play and creative approaches:

- Help to build resilience and nurture imagination and resourcefulness

- Establish a relationship of trust through the activity. The activity is an important focus and the relationship that is built is a by-product of this. This is especially helpful when working with damaged, isolated and alienated children and young people

- Promote awareness of local cultures and cultural diversity, promote inclusion and create cohesive communities

- Develop boundaries and awareness of risk, and develop life skills including decision-making

- Foster opportunities to identify and develop interests and skills

- Make learning concrete for children and young people, including those with special educational needs

- Promote teamwork and group-building

- Contribute to learning and can be used to assess progress

- Counter popular myths; through the use of media including videos we are able to explore stories, misconceptions, beliefs and values

- Promote physical activity which helps to prevent obesity

- Can be used by trained therapists in therapeutic work with children and young people.

Increasing concerns about litigation and the need to safeguard children has encouraged some schools and local authorities to limit the number of opportunities for challenge and adventure. This is not helpful, particularly where children and young people are leading increasingly sedentary lives. Concerns with welfare must be balanced against a need for children and young people to experience challenge and risk as part of their development.

Schools can provide opportunities for play and creativity through everyday curricular activities such as Physical Education, Music, Drama, Writing, Art and Crafts, as well as extra-curricular activities such as lunchtime and after-school clubs. In addition, linking up with local sports clubs, universities and community groups, and providing opportunities for play and adventure through school trips and residentials, offers huge scope for promoting emotional health and well-being through new experiences and stimulating activities which facilitate individual challenge and achievement, as well as group-building and teamworking opportunities.

Staff who are interested to further develop their understanding of and skills in the role and uses of play with children could consider the range of courses offered through the Institute for Arts in Therapy and Education who run a master's programme. Education in Emotional Literacy for Children (for further details see the Useful resources and organisations).

Life Routes is a life skills programme supporting PSHE. It is part of the global Make A Connection programme. Based at the National Children's Bureau, Life Routes provides resources, training and support to develop young people's life skills in school and community settings, including pupil referral units.

The resource provides a flexible programme and encourages creative approaches using arts, drama and multimedia. As part of their Extended Schools Programme, Hackney Local Authority worked with Mouth That Roars[1] to develop life skills through learning multimedia work. Young people described the experience:

> It made me realise my potential to make a difference. (17-year-old)

> The project helped me communicate and articulate myself. (15-year-old)

Others used a range of techniques including group work, drama and arts. Talking at a national conference in March, three young men aged 16, who had been excluded from school and were in a pupil referral unit, described the impact of the programme. Summing up their presentation, speaking to an audience of 150 people, one of them said 'Well it [Life Routes] must work, I am here talking to you aren't I?'

Case study: Roots and Wings

Roots and Wings is a multifaceted arts based emotional literacy project at Chickenley Community Primary School in Yorkshire. The school is set in an area of high multiple deprivation. The project received external funding from Children's Fund Kirklees to employ artists to work with the children to promote health and well-being, personal development and, thence, academic achievement.

The project involves a number of different elements including arts activities where children learn to draw, paint and use different materials, create self-portraits, make (and sell) greetings cards, knit and sew, use drama and story telling (a summary of these is shown on pages 82–83). The range of activities has been developed both in response to the children's interests, skills and talents, and a theoretical framework based on Perry's work (Bruce, P.D., www.ChildTrauma.org), where the school is committed to offering opportunities for children to learn and develop core emotional and social skills to enable them to:

- Be a friend and form healthy attachments which promote learning
- Think before acting – developing life skills and the ability to self-regulate
- Join in and develop the capacity to join others and contribute to a group
- Think of others and be able to read cues from others and respond to their needs
- Accept differences and learn to value things that make people special and unique
- Respect themselves and others and learn to listen, compromise and co-operate

(Continued)

---

[1] For more information visit www.mouththatroars.com.

(Continued)

The project also aims to create new traditions and rituals for the school and has developed a 'Roots and Wings Annual Carnival Parade' to support children through the transition from primary to secondary school (see pages 33–34 for further information).

Mary Robson, project co-ordinator, and Lesley Finnegan, head teacher, at the school are clear the key to the projects success is

- The development of strong positive relationships with adults and peers (this was also supported by the evaluation with pupils reporting: 'Best thing was working with Mary and Nicola; Mary and Nicola were always there for us; Mary helped me calm down.)'
- Multidisciplinary involvement
- A whole-school commitment to the process
- Children's active participation and commitment to the work and the leadership they offered

The first phase independent evaluation demonstrated significant successes in a number of key areas including:

- Motivation –   'I want to get all my lessons better – if my art can improve, so can the rest of my work' (Pupil)

- Concentration –   'It makes me concentrate more, because I am in a better mood (Pupil);

    'Everyone enjoys it, they are a lot calmer, more relaxed' (Teacher)

- Language usage and emotional development –   'My painting expresses loneliness, sadness and love. I used greens, oranges and blues. I think people should feel love and sadness' (Pupil);

    'I felt great when I did it. I felt passionate' (Pupil);

    'This work makes me happy – when I walk in, and welcome. It's the feelings room. There's loads of fantastic work up'

- Attendance –   'It made me come to school more, and I liked coming to school' (Pupil);

    'Because we see Mary – the artists wave at us' (Pupil)

- Confidence with peers and adults –   'My confidence has grown up to here' (hands high in the air) (Pupil);

    'I speak out now, I'm not so shy now' (Pupil)

- Ability to co-operate and work with others –   'You get to share ideas with other people' (Pupil);

    'I like working together and finding out new things' (Pupil)

The evaluator concluded: 'There are many exceptional stories of personal development and growth emerging from the Chickenley Kids Arts Project, and all of them point to a life-changing inspirational experience which these children find in the studio at Chickenley Community.'

Out of the box: providing new experiences and supporting talents

Our learning and emotional development is inspired by igniting curiosity; finding out what interests us and having stimulating experiences that make us feel and capture our imagination. For many children the home and family environment provides some of these experiences. Yet many others do not have this kind of home environment. For these children and young people school provides a view into the range of possibilities that are available for them. It also sends a clear signal that they are valued as members of the school community.

Schools therefore have a vital role in providing these experiences through lunchtime and extra-curricular activities, as well as school trips and activities planned as part of one-to-one personal development plans. Building the relationship is crucial as it allows us to learn what may interest children and young people and then to develop creative approaches and partnerships to respond imaginatively to these interests and desires.

Case study: Life Routes

A young man involved in Life Routes (the life skills programme managed by the National Children's Bureau as part of the global Make a Connection programme funded by Nokia) described the impact of new experiences.

He had been excluded from school for his behaviour and was part of a pupil referral unit. As part of his experience at the PRU staff identified that he was particularly interested in trains and wanted to become a train driver.

To help him achieve his goal, providing motivation and practical experience, the workers secured work experience at the local train station. Through the experience, Peter's commitment and determination to achieve his goal was reinforced and his effort in other areas increased.

Case study: The Young People's Development Programme

The Young People's Development Programme is a pilot funded by the Department of Health and the Department for Education and Skills. It aims to provide a range of activities and opportunities for young people to gain new experiences, develop emotional resilience and reduce risk-taking behaviours.

During the pilot phase there are nearly 30 projects each with different foci. Pilot projects include projects focusing on motivating skills and mentor-related activities, sports, adventure, arts and media activities. The projects also provide educational programmes, which build young people's self-esteem and confidence, skills in coping with feelings, managing risk, holding beliefs and giving/getting support.

The programme is being evaluated by the Institute of Education, University of London. Further information about the Young People's Development Programme is available at www.nya.org.uk.

Creative approaches to promoting emotional literacy

Providing creative opportunities for children and young people to develop a vocabulary for describing different feelings and, over time, progressing through to understanding what happens to their bodies when they are experiencing different feelings, recognising how feelings affect behaviour and learning positive strategies for using their thinking skills and feelings together to guide their behaviour. Examples of how to do this include:

■ Creating collages displaying people experiencing a range of emotions and feelings. This can be a trigger for discussion about how people feel and how they behave as a result of their feelings

■ Developing an A–Z of feelings, where each letter of the alphabet is written in columns down the side of a flip chart and in small groups asking pupils to think of a different feeling for each letter (creativity should be encouraged for some letters)

■ Playing 'feeling' charades in Drama, where pupils are given an emotion to act and the group has to guess what the feeling or emotion is. This can be a lead into further discussion about the relationships between how we feel and our verbal and non-verbal communication

■ Watching extracts from films or television programmes and being asked questions for discussion on the basis of the situation they have seen

■ Using scenarios and situations such as those provided in Cards for Life (see case study on page 56 and in useful resources and organisations) which enable children and young people to explore real-life situations which are like theirs, but through the third person. Done well these can help develop empathy and an awareness of the impact of feelings and behaviour

■ Using puppets and other drama-based approaches including role play to explore situations from different perspectives

■ Using arts-based approaches such as developing a wall-sized feelings chart where pupils are provided with headings for the chart such as:

– When people feel sad they might
– When people feel excited they might
– When people feel angry they might
– When people feel happy they might

■ Then in each column ask them to list all the behaviours that people might display if they are feeling one of these emotions. Use this as trigger to explore the issue, for example ask them:

– Whether it is easy or difficult to talk about how they feel and manage their feelings and whether it is important to do so

- Why some people might find it easier than others, for example are there any gender differences or cultural differences?
- To identify whether some behaviours are the same even if the emotions are different and if this is the case why

A school worked with a group of children with emotional and behavioural difficulties on feelings and emotions using puppets. Through the puppets the children and young people were able to explore and discuss emotions in lively and creative ways. Making the puppets, developing scenarios and situations, and then acting out the scenes provided a starting point through which they could discuss their own emotions and feelings.

KEY POINTS

- Play and opportunities for adventure and new experiences are a vital part of schooling
- Creativity engages people in different ways and can unleash fantasy and tuition enabling children and young people to connect with their feelings
- There are a number of creative approaches which through their content and process promote emotional and social development

CHAPTER 8

Pastoral support and access to services

School provision for one-to-one advice and support for accessing this support in the community is at least as important as curriculum provision. This chapter outlines some of the key opportunities that are available. It includes:

- An overview of peer support
- Advice on responding to critical events
- Provision of and referral to one to one advice and support

Peer support

McLaughlin and Alexander (2004) emphasise the importance of peer relationships, they draw on an analysis of research into adolescence and social change and argue that peer relationships and interactions are of increasing importance for adolescence. They assert that schools are a key site for supporting the development of constructive peer relationships and that the existing emphasis on peer support should continue (Mclaughlin and Alexander, 2004: 12).

Peer support is an umbrella term for a range of activities where children and young people are involved. It is based on the premise that children and young people have a strong desire to support each other and that they have significant influence amongst their peers (Hartley-Brewer, 2002). Peer support harnesses this positive influence through a wide range of activities, including:

- Peer education – children and young people are trained in different health issues such as mental health, sexual health, drugs or healthy eating. Often peer educators are slightly older than those who they are educating or have common characteristics such as belonging to a particular ethnic group

- Peer listening – where children and young people are trained and supported to listen to others who 'self-refer' to peer listeners. Peer listeners are often allocated a safe space within the school, which is well publicised so children know where to go and the type of help they will receive

- ■ Peer mentoring – children and young people help each other in a range of ways, it may be mentoring to develop self-confidence or an ability to work in a group, or mentoring in a particular area such as reading

- ■ Peer buddying – this is where children act as buddies to their peers. Buddies may be assigned to children and young people who are new to a school, or where someone has been bullied, as a way of 'reintegrating' and supporting them back into friendship circles

- ■ Peer research – is where children and young people are trained as researchers to explore particular issues. They can undertake surveys in the school about bullying, or find out whether children and young people would feel safe and confident in accessing help and support within the school

- ■ Peer mediation – takes place when children and young people are trained to defuse interpersonal disagreements between peers, including name-calling, bullying, fighting and quarrelling. 'Mediation is a structured process in which a neutral third party assists voluntary participants to resolve their dispute' (Stacey, 1996).

- ■ Peer advocacy – takes place when children and young people seek to identify and represent the views and interests of, or speak on behalf of, other children and young people. It is now government policy to ensure that the experience and reactions of children and young people as consumers is heard across all public services, including schools. Many schools already have school councils.

Principles of effective peer support

- ■ Children and young people are central and drive peer support programmes.

- ■ Peer support is part of a whole school approach, which promotes a positive and supportive ethos.

- ■ Peer support involves the active commitment of more than one staff member.

- ■ Children and young people are offered opportunities to develop the skills to support each other more effectively.

- ■ The self-esteem and emotional development of children and young people is nurtured.

- ■ Confidentiality and child protection issues are covered in training and all involved are clear about boundaries and referral procedures.

- ■ Clear objectives, boundaries and ground rules are established with the children and young people involved in peer support.

- ■ The selection criteria for peer supporters should be clear, publicised, fair and achievable.

- ■ Equal opportunities must apply to all children and young people wishing to become involved, and support must be available to make access possible.

(Continued)

(Continued)

■ All parents and carers should be kept informed of the project, their child's role in it and the skills they are developing.

■ Projects should be continuously monitored and evaluated to ensure that objectives are being met and principles adhered to.

■ Children and young people are to receive appropriate initial and ongoing training, support and supervision.

■ Those training children and young people must be suitably qualified and security checked.

■ There is liaison with local and national agencies who support peer initiatives.

Source: Parsons and Blake (2004).

Responding to critical moments and events

Within any school year there will be a number of events or critical moments, which can cause alarm, upset, disquiet or discomfort within the school. This may be:

■ A school-based event such as the death or serious injury of a pupil, a significant community member or a member of staff

■ A community-based event such as the closing down of a major place of employment which impacts on family lives

■ An external event such as the recent terrorist acts which have led in some communities and schools to increased levels of Islamaphobia

How these types of events are responded to will determine how children and young people cope with that particular incident or the issues that may re-surface that have not been addressed sufficiently well in the past and potentially contribute to setting a blueprint for how critical moments in their lives are addressed in the future.

Responding well includes:

■ Acknowledging what has happened and expressing sadness, anger or other feelings and, where relevant, the unacceptability of the situation

■ Containing, calming or regulating any extreme emotional responses in ways that help children see the situation in proportion and feel that their safety is not compromised

■ Involving children, young people and staff in deciding how the school community would like to address the situation and communicating decisions about how it will be responded to

- Providing opportunities for one-to-one support and further access to specialist services for those who may need additional support

- Where you have knowledge of children and young people who have particular experiences or situations, which means it may be having a big impact, take proactive action and offer them the opportunity to talk or get further support

---

Case study: Managing bereavement[1]

Winston's Wish, an agency providing bereavement support for children and young people, has developed the following hypothetical case study for schools to help them provide appropriate support to a child or young person coming back to school after experiencing a bereavement.

The pupil, Jason, is 10 years old and he returns to school three days after the unexpected death of his father. The case study sets out the steps that could helpfully be taken.

When the school is informed of the death

Jason's class teacher (Mr Lee) is informed and arrangements made for someone to cover his class for registration so he can develop a response plan. The rest of the staff are informed. It is agreed how pupils will be told, and previously bereaved children are identified in case they need extra support.

A letter is written for pupils to take home to their parents. Additional information is provided for Jason's classmates, which outlines possible reactions and responses from children. This includes helpline support. A letter of condolence is sent to Jason's family.

Before Jason returns to school

Staff are encouraged to acknowledge the death to and with Jason, and to talk with their class about how Jason and his family may be feeling and how they will support him on his return. Pupils explore how they might respond to Jason. Jason's own class and group of friends have a session on feelings connected with loss and grief.

Mr Lee visits Jason at home to tell him what has been happening at school and inform him and his family of how the school has been told about his father's death. They agree what will happen on his return to school.

When Jason returns to school

Mr Lee is waiting when Jason arrives and they have some time together. Mr Lee checks that Jason is still happy with the plans for his return to class.

Jason and his teacher identify an adult supporter for him. He is told that he can leave lessons to seek out his chosen supporter when he needs to. Jason and his teacher rejoin the rest of the class and carry out their 'return plan'.

Time is set aside at the end of the day for Jason to spend with Mr Lee, checking out how things have been during the day and to agree a plan for the following morning.

(Continued)

---

[1] Reproduced from *Spotlight* Issue One (December 2003) with permission from the National Children's Bureau.

(Continued)

Before the funeral

It is agreed with Jason's family how the school will mark the funeral and any school cere-mony. The school ensures that Jason's family knows about any local child bereavement service and also provides information on national services and supports referrals.

Mr Lee compiles a 'calendar of memories' noting any dates where Jason may need extra support – for example, the anniversary of the death, his father's birthday and Father's Day. This calendar can follow Jason through the school and on to his next school. Jason and his family agree with the school over marking Father's Day and other family occasions.

All those who teach Jason identify any areas of heightened sensitivity – for example, if his father died in a fire, studying the Great Fire of London will be difficult.

The head teacher uses a future staff meeting to review events and the school's response, and to plan for any future bereavements.

One-to-one advice and support

Every Child Matters emphasises the importance of providing strong one-to-one advice and support as part of a commitment to improving well-being and life chances through early intervention. Many children and young people will at some point or another within their school career, need one-to-one advice and support to enable them to handle situations and circumstances either within school or outside school. Children can only learn well if they feel safe and happy amongst their peers and staff. Providing well for this one-to-one support is crucial to improving behaviour and raising standards. Schools respond best when they have formed strong partnerships with professionals who work within the school context and in the community.

All children and young people need access to someone who they can discuss issues with in private, knowing that the adult they talk to will listen to them and take their situation seriously. In some schools this will be a class teacher or form tutor. In others it may be a school nurse, a learning mentor or a personal adviser. Support staff in schools such as learning mentors, Connexions advisers and teaching assistants have a particularly helpful role to play in providing this type of one-to-one support (Cooper, 2005). Who provides the support is less important than the fact that children and young people know who to go to and that their needs are being taken and responded to seriously.

Some children and young people will need support which is more substantial or 'expert'. There are different levels and types of one-to-one advice and support that sit along a continuum. These include:

- Providing proactive opportunities for those children and young people recognised as vulnerable. Many learning mentors provide art and other creative opportunities where children and young people develop their confidence and self-esteem and form posi-tive relationships

   – Some schools provide peer support opportunities for those children and young people who are experiencing loss or separation. Voluntary lunchtime and after-school activities which provide a place to go and provide peer support have proven helpful for children at both secondary and primary school

■ Ensuring one-to-one advice in the school is available through school nursing, learning mentors, peer supporters or a school counsellor

■ Signposting and referring children and young people to sources of help and support including voluntary agencies, websites, phone lines and community services

■ Referring directly or encouraging parents and carers to seek referrals to educational psychologists, child and adolescent mental health services and voluntary organisations that provides advice and support

■ Providing health services on the school site in partnership with health. When mental health services are available in schools, they are highly effective and, as such, government suggests that educational psychologists and child adolescent mental health workers should offer training and support to schools in this area (DH, 2004)

KEY POINTS

■ All children and young people need access to private advice which they know how to access and feel confident accessing

■ Providing effective one-to-one support is crucial to promote self-esteem, health and learning

■ Peer support is a robust vehicle for developing positive supportive relationships

CHAPTER 9

Professional development

This chapter offers:

- Activities that can be used in a half day INSET session or twilight sessions with staff
- A brief overview of best practice in training in this area
- Accompanying notes for staff which can be copied and handed out to participants in the training session

The activities are a sequence of sessions that can either precede the whole-school audit (see Chapter 3) or can be carried out as a response to the needs identified in the audit.

The promotion of emotional health and well-being is a whole-staff responsibility and therefore all staff within the school including administrative staff are helpfully involved in professional development activities. These INSET activities are designed to be an introduction, aiding whole-school reflection. More specialist training and support is available from a range of agencies. See Useful resource and organisations for further information.

Staff development in emotional health and well-being is sometimes different to other training because one of the main things teachers need to learn is that *learning about* is only part of the task. For example, if the topic of work is 'Friendship', part of the work may be looking at 'what qualities do you look for in a friend?' (drawing on the cognitive part of ourselves), but what is of key importance is actually experiencing the relationship – being 'in' the relationship and then using that to understand our feelings towards different people, our preferences, prejudices and so on. It may be more difficult to manage a group of children who are being 'real' about relationships (peers, teachers, parents) and actually contacting different feelings as compared to completing a friendship questionnaire.

Setting staff tasks and following up the work with well-thought-out questions designed to get at the feelings the teachers are experiencing may lead to in-depth discussion and help them to identify the difficulties they may find in this type of learning.

'Experiential learning' (Stanford, 1990) is crucial as it enables emotions to be an explicit part of the process and learning. Invite the staff group to:

1 *Experience an activity* – actually do something (for example, find five different people in the training group who have similar hobbies to you)

2 When the activity is over, ask staff to *describe briefly what happened*: what did they do?

3 *Consider how they felt* about doing the activity (for example, did they find it easy/hard/ interesting/boring. *Note: Any* answer is fine – accentuate individual difference. It is important to communicate that there is not a right or wrong answer. People may offer 'thinking' responses, for example, 'I thought "not another ice-breaker". Link their responses to the four core feelings – happy, sad, scared, angry – 'So how did you feel when you thought that? Of the four core feelings, which was the closest: angry? Or scared?'

4 *Consider what they have learned* from the exercise so far (for example, 'Although I don't like doing ice-breakers, I can really see the importance of them', 'I realised how often I put pupils into situations that may cause them anxiety', and so on)

5 *Consider how can they apply what they have learned* (for example, 'I will think twice before asking some pupils to do certain activities – I will make sure they have support')

Engaging in such an activity may help staff understand what learning from the experience means. It may also help staff to understand the important part emotions play in all learning.

The following notes for staff have been prepared as a source of background information for the trainer to use as a basis for a presentation or as a handout for participants. The activities follow the notes for staff.

It is essential, for the success of this training, that the activities are planned in a way that provides a safe environment in which effective learning can take place. This is done by:

■ Making it clear at the beginning of each activity what is going to happen and what people are going to do, and by ensuring that expectations and concerns are explored and addressed

■ Setting working agreements (for example, about confidentiality, or avoiding personal questions or disclosures)

■ Being aware of, and responding to, the different needs and backgrounds of the participants, and taking time to build group trust and cohesion

■ Observing and responding appropriately to group dynamics

■ Summarising at regular intervals, to help the group feel 'contained' and 'safe'

■ Giving opportunities for reflection, encouragement and support

■ Evaluating and assessing the activities to help participants reflect on them and identify what they have learnt.

The activities each have a title, introduction, an estimate of the overall time required a list of the materials, and a step-by-step method.

NOTES FOR STAFF

1: Emotions, brain development and behaviour[1]

Relationship

Infants first develop their sense of themselves in relation to and with key adults. The care they receive directly influences the development of neural pathways in the brain. This in turn determines how the brain responds to strong emotions and the behaviours that we use to manage them.

The early experiences of depending on a 'significant other' (often called 'attachment', Bowlby, 1969) colour the ways we learn to think about ourselves in relation to the world. The quality of this relationship is central to children's emotional health and well-being. Their brains become 'hard-wired' for particular responses *until or unless* other significant experiences establish the brain capacity for something different to happen.

Children's experience *in* relationship and *of* relationship is key to their brain development, the unfolding of their personality, their emotional development and their perceptions, core beliefs and sense of identity. Experience shows that some children and young people in schools will not have had positive relationships, and life events will have contributed to them having largely negative experiences of adults and authority. This will negatively impact on their emotional health and well-being. It is important that any school takes this into account, as well as acknowledging, supporting and extending those pupils whose experience is much more positive. All pupils' needs must be recognised and met.

Significant others

The child remembers the quality of the emotional interactions s/he has with the key care-provider(s). The child learns what to expect and makes sense of her/his world accordingly. In this way, s/he learns:

- How to be

- Who s/he is and how to respond to what goes on, in order to survive

When their experiences are 'good enough' the child develops trust and feels safe. This 'trust' is basic to emotional health and well-being. As the child grows, people other than the original care-givers contribute to the child's emotional health and well-being. By adolescence, for an emotionally healthy child, more attention is paid to relationships with other young people of the same age, as belonging to a group becomes more important. But for young people whose early development was interrupted, a stable, positive relationship with a reliable caring adult is needed before other productive relationships can be developed.

---

[1] Adapted with permission from Bird. J. and Gerlach. L. (2005) *Improving the Emotional Health and Well-being of Young People in Secure Care*. National Children's Bureau.

Hard-wiring the brain

When the baby/child more consistently experiences unpredictable, frightening, emotionally distant or abusive interactions, s/he expects relationships that are filled with:

- ■ Uncertainty

- ■ Fear

- ■ Anger

- ■ Distance

- ■ And distress

The world becomes an unsafe place. The 'alarm' circuits in her/his brain keep firing; instinctive responses of 'fight, flight, freeze' get hard-wired into the brain as neuronal pathways get established.

➜	fight		
➜	flight	➜	**no access to thinking**
➜	freeze		

The child's brain literally gets shaped by these experiences so that these children are more likely to experience rage, anxiety, fear, hatred and be less able to access thinking. The instinctive responses become habitual over time – 'the way we do things' – as the growing child learns how to manage her/him self in the family setting. When the family's way of doing things runs counter to the way wider society wants things done, this can develop into behaviour patterns that get the young person into trouble.

Loving, soothing interactions with primary care-givers, on the other hand, shape the brain for resilience to stress. Being soothed by someone who cares for you when you are distressed stimulates the chemical and hormonal reactions in the brain that develop neural pathways to calming and thinking.

> Soothing, loving interactions ➜ calm down and soothe the distressed child ➜ the child becomes able to self-soothe ➜ s/he can calm down and think when scared, angry, sad or anxious

If a child is going to learn to calm themselves down, they have to have experiences of being calmed down and soothed by someone who matters to them first. A young person who responds:

- ■ with aggression – for example shouting, hitting, pushing, punching, swearing

- ■ by controlling – for example dominating, needing to be in charge

- ■ by withdrawing – for example shutting down, running off, going silent

is behaving in the ways s/he knows to manage the situation s/he find her/himself in. They need to learn some new responses. This requires experiencing something different in relationship so they can learn new skills

For some children playtime is a nightmare. For an adult to acknowledge this with empathy while respecting the child's integrity and do something to remedy the situation will make such a difference to the child.

What does this mean for our practice in schools?

- Taking time to develop relationships with young people

- Paying attention, noticing details, valuing who they are

- Taking time to listen; offering spaces to talk

- Separating out the behaviour from the person

- Not taking their behaviours personally

- Using voice, pace and steadiness to calm and soothe a distressed young person

- Teaching other ways to manage strong feelings

- Giving information about alternative replacement behaviours; reinforcing them with praise and encouragement

Training activities for emotions, brain development and behaviour

Aim

To develop understanding of how relationships with significant others affect the hard-wiring of the brain which, in turn, has an impact on behaviour.

Intended outcomes

- To understand the importance of the relationship between pupils and staff in schools and how this affects the development of their emotional health and well-being.

- To develop ways of using the relationships between adult and child, child and child to provide experiences which promote positive emotional health and well-being.

Activity 1: The game of sabotage

Time: 45 minutes

Note: This activity is helpful in bringing to the surface negativity beginning real honest dialogue.

Method

1 Explain what *sabotage* means (to destroy, to distract attention away from task/activity).

2 Ask everyone to write down ways that they have sabotaged learning or working groups for themselves and others in the past (including when at school).

3 On their own, ask them to write down all the ways they can think of to sabotage the training session today. Then ask them to discuss with a partner.

4 Bring the whole group together so that they can share their ideas.

Discussion points

- Why do we engage in sabotage?

- How do you feel when adults in your group/organisation sabotage what is going on?

- How do you feel when young people engage in sabotage?

- What do you do when the young people sabotage themselves/others (activity and/or learning)?

- What can you positively contribute to today's training?

(Continued)

(Continued)

5   Use the Experiential Learning Cycle to conclude this activity:

■   What did you do? (that is, explain the procedure)

■   How did you feel?

■   What did you learn?

■   How will you apply what you have learned?

Activity 2: Active listening

Time: 30 minutes

Method

1   Ask people to get into pairs and to label themselves A or B.

2   Ask A to choose from one of the topics below, and to talk for 5 minutes while B listens. They should then swap around.

3   At the end, each person gives their partner constructive, specific feedback relating to what was good about their listening.

Choose from the following topics:

■   Who was/is a significant influence in your work in schools?

■   Why did you choose working with children as your career?

■   How did you learn to calm yourself when distressed?

■   What has helped you to learn to manage difficult/distressing emotions?

■   What behaviours do you use when you are stressed, anxious or scared?

■   What behaviours do you use when you are angry?

■   What differences have you noticed between the ways that men and women communicate being scared or sad?

4   Small group (4) feedback discussing 'What constitutes good listening?'

5   Whole group summarising what good listening involves, that is:

■   Paying good attention

■   Using body language that communicates acceptance and interest

■   Reflecting back what has been said to show you have heard accurately and understood

(Continued)

- Paraphrasing the essence of what has been said

- Using open-ended questions

- Using empathy; reading the feeling behind the words

- Summarising and checking you have understood.

Activity 3: Discussing Notes for Staff 1

Time: 45 minutes

Resources

- Copies of Notes for Staff 1

Method

1 Arrange for each group member to have time to read and consider Notes for Staff 1.

2 Ask people to get into groups of three or four to discuss the contents of the paper and their reactions to it:

- What are the most interesting and important points for them?

- What are the implications for their practice?

- What do they do well? Consider personal practice and practice as a team

- What, if anything, do they want to change in their own practice?

- What changes might it be good to make to their workplace policies and practice?

- What support do they need to do this?

NOTES FOR STAFF

2: Developing emotional health and well-being – a job for life

As they grow, children have different learning jobs – for example, to learn to trust, to learn about safety and their own physical capabilities, to learn language and be able to communicate, to learn about rules and internalise values and to learn various skills. Research confirms that human beings continue to have useful developmental experiences throughout life. Providing we get the right opportunities, and the support to make good use of them, we can go on developing. Learning really is lifelong.

We *can* make up for lost or missing experiences and we *can* experience anew – and we do this in relationship with the people who matter to us and by having chances to learn what we need to learn next.

When we face transitions or losses, our earliest needs to be safe and cared for get triggered.

A Year 6 pupil, Jade, had experienced cumulative losses as a young child. The school recognised her vulnerability and placed her in an ENABLE group at her primary school where Jade learned to feel safe, special and was learning to meet her own needs. Her relationships with the ENABLE co-ordinator and a learning support assistant in the school had really developed in the previous two years and she has begun to trust adults. Going to secondary school presented a major difficulty. Jade's behaviour deteriorated. The staff at the school recognised the difficulty and put in a number of strategies to support Jade at this very difficult time. One of the successful strategies for Jade was to have a weekly drop-in session with the ENABLE co-ordinator at the primary school, which coincided with children returning home from secondary school. This 'bridge' between primary and secondary schools is very important for a child such as Jade. She is learning that there will be support available in the familiar place and that change/transition is hard for all of us and CAN BE PREPARED FOR and REHEARSED.

Interruptions to development can put emotional health and well-being at risk. The pupils in school whose behaviour causes the most distress have rarely had an easy, supportive childhood. The following experiences are likely to put their emotional development – and their mental health – at risk.

Inconsistent or punishing attention

Neglect

Being abandoned

Harshness, humiliation or hostility

Cruelty

(Continued)

Abuse

Chaos/unpredictability

Poverty

Discrimination/harassment

Separation from parents/carers

Grief complications

Alcohol or drug misuse

Ill health in family (mental, emotional or prolonged physical illness)

Providing what is needed developmentally

Schools can and do play a crucial part in providing the developmental experiences that children and young people need. At different times in our lives we have different emotional developmental tasks in order to develop in an emotionally healthy way. Staff in schools need to be aware of these different tasks in order to give pupils appropriate developmentally needed experiences when children's development has been interrupted.

Desirable experiences	This includes things like	In a school this might look like
Being safe	Having others look out for and look after you before you can do it for yourself and when you can't do it for yourself Having boundaries Having basic needs cared for Knowing you are in safe hands	Secure, risk-assessed sites Consistent, caring supervision A few simple clearly explained rules Routines; clear expectations that can be met Support when you need it Places, times and people you can go to for help
Being significant	Being valued and accepted Being noticed Being prized and celebrated Being listened to Influencing outcomes. Being supported to take responsibility for achievable outcomes with increasing independence over time	'Star of the day' – events to be the focus of positive attention Positive relationships with staff and peers Positive interactions with others Rewards and recognition systems Opportunities to have special responsibilities and to participate in decision-making, for example about the way the unit is run

(Continued)

Desirable experiences	This includes things like	In a school this might look like
Experiencing and exploring our physical presence, experience and environment	Safe physical exploration Getting to know your own body and its strengths and limits Being able to explore the environment safely Experiencing action and feeling over time to understand continuity Exploring, trying out, testing, 'risking safely'	Soft play spaces, sensory trails, outdoor facilities/experiences and games; sport and challenge activities; adventure/challenge areas; ponds, natural or wild areas; opportunities to play and experiment with sand, water, clay, paints, crayons; toys and or equipment to learn gross motor skills and improve co-ordination
Exploring with others our feelings, intentions, experiences, values	Being watched, listened to, having emotions named Reading body language Intonation and gesture Sharing a focus of attention Recognising feeling states in ourselves and others. Talking, listening, reflecting	Activities to learn about feelings, develop a 'feelings vocabulary', experience and develop empathy; circle time; debates, discussions; opportunities to talk and be listened to; effective group work This can be developed in Sex and Relationships and Drugs education, Citizenship education; PSHE
Exploring symbolic play and creativity on our own and with others	Recognising and using signs, symbols, image and metaphor Being self-reflective Describing your reality Developing shared meanings and a shared narrative (ways of talking about what happens)	Story; storytelling, drama, role play, language, images, metaphor, music, art, literature, dance, mime, movement that communicates about feelings, meanings and experiences
Developing and extending a range of emotional, social and behavioural skills over time	Having opportunities to learn the next skills, understanding or knowledge/insight you need	Taught courses to develop relationship skills, emotional literacy, conflict resolution, negotiating skills, independent living skills; thinking skills, leadership qualities, and so on; group work like circle time
Developing an internal structure of values and principles that contributes to way(s) of making sense of our experience and informs our actions	Having opportunities to explore, talk about, listen to others, discuss and debate values and principles Having role models who demonstrate values and principles in action	Religious education; moral education; values and rights education; Philosophy for Children; meditation; PSHE; Citizenship education

Never too late to learn

The challenge for teachers and support staff who are working with young people whose emotional development has been interrupted is to provide the needed experiences in ways that are age-appropriate. Young people do not want to be exposed in front of their peers. They do not want to be shown up or labelled. They do, however, need in the current time some of the experiences that others may have had much earlier in their lives. Some potentially important reparative experiences are:

■ Play: physical exploration and challenge

■ Recognising emotional cues through facial expressions, gesture, intonation, and so on

■ Being able to depend on someone else to have their needs met

■ Have a place and things of their own

■ Understand about rules, boundaries and limits

■ Basic relational skills

■ Having their experience recognised, named and accepted

■ Learning ways to share, take turns; sometimes to lead, sometimes to follow

■ Having someone provide a positive running commentary of their actions

■ Doing things alongside someone else

Of great importance is *how* this is done. The adult involved in this work must like the child (see the person beyond the behaviour), have the capacity to empathise with the child/young person and be able to contain them and set the emotional tone rather than allowing the young person to dominate.

Training activities for emotional health and well-being – a job for life

Aim

To develop understanding of how young people's different developmental needs can be addressed.

Intended outcomes

- To be better able to recognise and name emotions.

- To begin to develop a feelings vocabulary.

- To explore ways of meeting children/young people's developmental needs in their provision.

Activity 1: Naming emotions

Introduction

Developing a language of emotions that enables us to describe our feelings is an essential step towards recognising and managing feelings. When a child or young person has had an earlier experience of good attachment with his/her carers (when the child has been attuned to, loved, prized, valued, has had their needs met and has been kept safe), and when he/she has had their feelings noticed, accepted and talked about by putting a name to the internal experience – 'I'm guessing you are sad when you talk about that?' – the child has the foundations for the language of feelings. If this has not been the child's experience, adults around the child have to do this reparative work with the child/young person before the child will notice they are getting angry let alone say 'I need some help – I am about to lose my temper'! The reparative process is:

- *Welcoming, accepting, commenting and caring* about the child (meeting the child as they enter the room and saying 'hello' and really looking at them and noticing them 'I like your hair')

- *Empathising* with the child and trying to read what is going on 'You look a bit lost, let me show you where to go' … 'I get scared when I'm in a new place – is that how it is for you?'

- *Externalising* what you think is going on for them. Children who cannot communicate in words how they feel (but can only do it through their behaviour) need us to guess what their internal reality is and name it for them. If we get it wrong – it does not matter – they will tell us. By us externalising their inner experience, the child feels understood (attuned to) and will start the process of being able to name it for themselves.

- *Explaining the physical experience of feelings* ('When I am scared I get a fluttery feeling in my chest, my breathing gets shallow and so on – what happens to you in your body?')

If a child does not have an emotional language, this reparative work must happen before he/she will be able to do the exercise below.

(Continued)

> As well as developmental differences, language is personal: one person's 'cross' is another person's 'furious'. Accept and explore the differences. There are lots of words to describe feelings and within any group the same word may have slightly different meanings for different members. Work out from the language that you use every day the words you know young people use to describe the same emotion.

For adults who are not confident in talking about emotions, it can help to begin the exploration by using images, pictures, photographs, video clips and/or arts media like stories, puppets, painting, drawing, collage, play-dough, clay or sand trays with figures.

Time: 55 minutes

Resources

- Flip-chart paper and pens

- Photographs, pictures, video clips, extracts from films and television programmes (especially 'soaps') can be used as a stimulus to explore and discuss the relationship between people's body language (posture, gestures, expressions, intonation, and so on) and their feelings; and the relationship between feelings and different behaviours

Method

1. Ask everyone to get into pairs. Using pictures and/or photographs of babies, children and adults in different situations, ask everyone to select a picture of a person, and discuss with their partner the following:

   (a) Describe how the person looks (for example face muscles tense, looking down, shoulders back)
   (b) Can they tell how the person feels from the description?
   (c) From the description, can they work out how the person feels?
   (d) How did they come to that decision?
   (e) What were the clues that they picked up?

2. Ask everyone to form a circle. Everyone should take it in turns to enter the circle communicating a feeling by body language, gesture or movement and sound only. After each person has their turn, everyone else mimics the same movements. *Remember there is always a right to pass.*

3. On a piece of flip-chart paper, write the headings *happy, scared, sad, angry* and *worried*. Ask the whole group to suggest words that describe these feelings, and write them up under the headings. (Use the words that you and the group use currently and then add the words that young people use.)

(Continued)

(Continued)

Discussion points

- How do we first learn the words that describe feelings?

- Do you find it easy to describe your feelings?

- Do the young people with whom you work find it easy to describe their feelings?

- Is it important that you can describe *and* talk about your feelings?

- Is it important that the young people can use words that describe their feelings? Give reasons why/why not.

- What is the step-by-step process that we learn to understand and manage feelings, and where in this process does naming emotions occur?

Activity 2: Discussing Notes for Staff 2

Time: 45 minutes

Resources

- Copies of Notes for Staff 2

Method

1   Arrange for each group member to have time to read and consider Notes for Staff 2.

2   Ask people to work in small groups of three to discuss the contents of the paper and their reactions to it:

- What are the most interesting and important points?

- What are the implications for practice?

- What are they doing well?

- What, if anything, do they want to change in their own practice?

- What changes might it be good to make to their workplace policies and practice?

- What support do they need to do this?

The next Notes for Staff and related activities are for those working in and with secondary schools as the focus is on the particular emotional health and well-being issues and developmental tasks for adolescents.

Notes for staff 3:

Understanding emotional development in young people

Jean Illesley-Clarke and Connie Dawson (1989) identified that adolescents and young adults have three key developmental tasks:

■ to become confident in their sexual identity

■ to become independent of adults

■ to take their place in an independent world where they can give and receive support as appropriate

At the same time they are also recycling all the earlier developmental needs that as yet have not been sufficiently well addressed.

Case study: A special case ...

Barry has real difficulty with his peers and he is uncommunicative with his key worker. Left to explore the materials in the craft room, he gets really involved with making a collection of fabrics with different textures.

He does not 'do' anything with them but enjoys feeling them and arranging them in patterns. Realising that he is likely to get teased by his peers for this behaviour, a worker works with him to make a fabric holdall to keep the collection somewhere safe. It is the first time his special things have been recognised.

Psychologists, including Berne (1973), have identified that all human beings, if they are to be fully healthy and able to function well in society, need 'good enough' experiences of the following:

■ *touch:* non-intrusive contact

■ *sensory stimulation:* visual, auditory, kinaesthetic, tactile and spaces for 'chilling' as well as stimulation

■ *recognition:* comments, looks, smiles, acknowledgement, praise, applause, attention, being valued

■ *structure:* known, predictable routines; plans that are followed through; recognition and celebration of special events in the yearly cycle; order; personalised spaces

■ *incident/drama:* exciting, new, out of the ordinary, the unknown, challenge and risk

■ *acceptance as a potential or actual sexual being:* acknowledgement of arousal, attraction; physical needs

■ *spirituality:* experience of deep connection, wonder at life, have an urge to find meaning, share a very special moment with another/others; make sense of the unfathomable, experience connection to a life force greater than themselves

Young people who have not had enough attention, positive notice, valuing, safe touch and safe excitement sometimes substitute sexual activity in an effort to get those earlier more basic needs met. Where sexual contacts are putting the young person emotionally or physically at risk, increase your attention to addressing their other basic needs.

Creative challenges

Young people have a particularly strong need for incident and stimulation. They need bright colours, loud and exciting noises, physical challenges, new social contacts, opportunities for socialising, fun, drama, 'special' events, trips out, and numerous opportunities to participate, to get involved in taking responsibility, for using initiative and taking charge. It is a challenge to staff's creativity to meet their developmental needs in ways that keep them safe and do not put them at excessive risk, whilst offering fun, excitement and challenge. Leadership courses and outward-bound challenges are helpful.

From his work with severely traumatised young people, Hughes (2002) suggests a variety of strategies for meeting the needs of these young people (see below).

Getting a buzz from life

To help young people increase their capacity for fun, love and connection:

1 Communicate that you recognise and understand the feeling the young person is experiencing

2 Stay physically close

3 Get to know (and do something about) you own issues from your early history

4 Use eye contact, smiles, touch, rocking, movement, food

5 Be emotionally available in times of stress

6 Provide good surprises

7 Agree and use safe touch, for example, holding the young person

8 Make choices for the young person and structure their activities

9 Be willing to communicate your thoughts and feelings reciprocally

10 Use humour and gentle, affectionate teasing

11 Maintain basic safety and security at all times

12 At times, play the 'good' parent figure

13 Be available for spontaneous discussion of past and future

14 Create routines and rituals to develop a mutual history, for example, have a special time once a week (or month or year) when you do something together, such as having a special meal on an anniversary of a success, or ask the young person to be responsible

---

(Continued)

for something as part of how you do things together. This way they get to feel special, trusted and responsible

15 Create memory books or portfolios of achievements

16 As and when the young person can manage it successfully, create opportunities for them to successfully participate

Staying in the clear

To help staff maintain effective discipline and help the young person to develop self-discipline:

1 Stay physically close

2 Make choices for the young person and structure their activities

3 Set and maintain your favourite emotional tone, not the young person's

4 Accept the thoughts, feelings and behaviours of the young person

5 Provide natural and logical consequences of behaviour

6 Be predictable in your attitude, that is, accepting, curious, interested, committed

7 Be less predictable in your consequences: avoid lecturing or boring repetition of the same points or always giving a predictable task in response to something having gone wrong

8 Reconnect emotionally soon after things have gone wrong; provide corrective emotional repair

9 Be available for close company, especially when the young person is resistant; stay quietly present

10 Use paradoxical responses, such as 'Wow, that was loud – could you do it louder?'

11 Demonstrate thinking; support practising or rehearsing; have clear limits

12 Employ quick, appropriate anger, not habitual anger or annoyance: '60-second scolding'; use 'I' messages not 'you' or 'everyone' (for example, 'I was shocked' rather than 'You feel shocked' or 'Everyone's shocked' when actually describing your own response – This models taking responsibility for your own feelings and behaviour); give information, then quickly change manner; communicate empathy and a continued connection; reassure, give a hug/touch if possible

13 Clarify for all concerned that it is the young person's problem not your problem

14 Reciprocate communication of thoughts and feelings

15 Be in charge, but also be attuned to the feelings of the young person

16 Greatly limit the young person's ability to hurt you, either physically or emotionally

17 Get to know and address your own issues from your early 'attachment' history

Training activities for staff

Aim

To develop understanding of how to make best provision for young people

Intended outcomes

- To aid staff to explore the ways in which their relationships with young people can be better used to promote and develop emotional health and well-being

- To explore the ways in which provision could be improved to better address the needs of young people

---

Activity 1: Making our relationships with young people more significant

Introduction

Considering what opportunities there are to forge and deepen relationships with and between young people forms the focus of this activity.

Time: 55 minutes

Resources:

- Copies of Notes for Staff 3

- Copies of 'Making relationships with young people more significant: action plan' (see page 110)

- Flip chart, stand and paper, marker pens A4 paper, Blu-Tack

Method

1 Ask everyone to work individually or with a partner in the same year group. Suggest they imagine the daily routine for one of the young people in their class. It is often helpful to choose a young person whose behaviour causes concern, or who is known to be vulnerable. (10 minutes)

2 Give everyone paper and pen. Ask them to chart the key events and all of the opportunities for positive interaction between staff member and young person. Encourage them to write down their thoughts and feelings about how the young person experiences him/herself in relation to staff. (15 minutes)

3 With a partner or in a small group, ask them to discuss their notes. You can prompt them with the following questions:

(Continued)

■ Who currently has good contact with this young person? What makes it good?

■ Who has an opportunity to make or enhance the current contact with this young person?

■ In what ways can this be done?

■ What and where are the most opportune moments for a relationship to be prioritised with (a) a significant adult and (b) peers?

■ What support do staff need to be able to work most effectively in a one-to-one relationship?

■ What, if anything, needs to be done for the improvement of relationships to be prioritised in your year group/class/subject area? Create an action plan (see handout on the following page).

MAKING RELATIONSHIPS WITH YOUNG PEOPLE MORE SIGNIFICANT: ACTION PLAN

Improving the quality of adult-young person relationships/interactions: POSSIBILITIES	Increasing the opportunities for more effective peer relationships: OPPORTUNITIES

Aim

To develop understanding of how to make best provision for young people.

Intended outcomes

- To aid staff in identifying for themselves how they get their basic emotional needs met

- To consider the ways in which your school currently addresses these needs for young people

- To explore the ways in which provision can be improved to better address the needs of young people

---

Activity 2: Discussing Notes for Staff 3

Introduction:

This activity allows the participants to familiarise themselves with essential research and key points about emotional development and young people.

Time: 45 minutes or to be read before training session

Resources:

- Copies of Notes for Staff 3

Method

1 Arrange for each member to have time to read the Notes for Staff (in or before the session). (15 minutes)

2 Ask people to discuss in small groups of three or four the contents of the paper and their reactions to it:

- What are the most interesting and important points?

- What are the implications for practice?

- What are they doing well?

- What, if anything, do they want to change in their own practice?

- What changes might it be good to make to their workplace policies and practice?

- What support do they need to do this?

Guidance and draft policy on the use of safe touch in schools

DRAFT GUIDANCE AND POLICY[1] ON 'SAFE TOUCH'.

The draft policy set out below is intended to inform you and guide your thinking about the development of your own school/workplace policy on the use of 'safe touch'. This is a sensitive and potentially controversial topic. We believe that learning and care communities need to consider this important topic in depth. If 'safe touch' is to be used it must be done with the full knowledge and consent of parents/carers, by trained and supervised staff in carefully monitored situations where its therapeutic use has been agreed because it addresses an identified developmental need on the part of the child. Schools and other learning or care situations need to develop a policy through a rigorous consultation process with all members of the community. The use of 'safe touch' by designated adults needs to be supervised, monitored and reviewed on a regular basis, as indeed does the policy, to ensure that it continues to meet the needs of children, parents/carers and staff.

THE DEVELOPMENTALLY NECESSARY EXPERIENCE OF SAFE TOUCH

INTRODUCTION

Children learn who they are and how the world is IN RELATIONSHIP. The quality of the child's relationships with significant adults is key to their healthy development and emotional health and wellbeing.

Research (see Appendix 2) shows clearly that healthy pro-social brain development requires access to *safe touch* as one of the means of calming, soothing and containing distress for a frightened, sad or angry child. It is essential for all children to learn the difference between safe and unsafe touch and to experience having their strongest emotions contained, validated, accepted and soothed by a significant adult. If children are behaving in unacceptable, threatening, dangerous, aggressive or out of control ways, they have not yet learned how their

---

[1] This guidance and draft policy was first created within the context of a specialist ENABLE project in a Primary School. Other schools wishing to adapt the policy would need to adapt it to fit their particular circumstances. The copyright of this policy is restricted to Sowelu Associates 2005

strongest emotional reactions can be contained, channelled and communicated safely. In recognition of this, *under special, agreed and supervised conditions*, specially trained staff will consider using *safe touch* as one of the means available to them for example to calm a distressed child, contain an angry or wild child and or encourage or affirm an anxious child or a child with low self esteem. *Safe touch* used to calm, soothe and regulate a child's emotions is a needed developmental experience. The brain does not develop self-soothing neuronal pathways unless and until this safe emotional-regulation has been experienced. Where children have had insufficient experience of *safe touch* and calming regulation this may be a priority to help the brain to develop access to thinking, judging and evaluating mechanisms. Safe touch is one of the key ways of regulating children's emotions but it is a strategy that *fully trained staff will use only under supervision and in line with a whole school Policy on Touch*. Other means of calming, soothing and containing children's strong emotions include:

- Slowing one's pace

- Lowering the voice

- Breathing more deeply

- Initially matching the pitch and volume of the child's emotional display (shout, cry etc) and then regulating it down

- Talking slowly, firmly and quietly in an unhurried unflustered way

- Providing clear, predictable, consistently held boundaries

Context

Our policy on Touch has been developed in the context of the LEA Child Protection Procedures and Policies. It takes into account the extensive neurobiological research and other empirical studies relating to attachment theory and child development that identify safe touch as a positive contribution to brain development, emotional regulation, mental health and the development of pro-social skills.

To whom does it apply:

All staff and children working within the specialist project/or pastoral team

Identified staff are trained by a specialist child psychotherapist/Education Inspector in the identification and use of safe touch as a developmental intervention. All of the staff team receive regular case supervision with a specialist Consultant and their day-to-day practice is monitored by the Project Co-ordinator and the Headteacher.

Why have a policy on touch?

In order to protect children and school staff from allegations under Child Protection procedures most schools and LEAs have adopted 'No Touch' policies. However this school is adopting an informed, evidence based decision to allow safe touch in special cases as a developmentally appropriate intervention that will aid healthy growth and learning.

Safe touch is one of the key ways of regulating children's emotions but it is a strategy that fully trained staff will use **only** under supervision and in line with the school's Policy on Touch.

The developmentally appropriate (and therapeutic) use of safe touch is defined by situations in which abstinence would actually be inhumane, unkind and potentially psychologically or neuro-biologically damaging. Examples include the empirically backed beneficial use of touch in the comforting of a child who is in an acute state of distress and/or out of control. Not to reach out to the child in such circumstances could be re-traumatising and neuro-biologically damaging, confirming or inviting anti-social behaviour patterns. Abstinence in the face of intense grief, stress and/or rage reactions can lead to a state of hyper-arousal, in which toxic levels of stress chemicals are released in the body and brain. The severely damaging long-term effects of this state have been intensively researched worldwide and are well documented.

Moreover, gentle safe holding is appropriate if a child:

- is hurting himself/herself or others, (or is likely to hurt himself/herself and/or others) or

- is damaging property, and/or

- is incensed and out of control, so that all verbal attempts to engage him/her have failed.

Such necessary interventions are fully in line with guidelines set out in the Government Document, 'New Guidance on the Use of Reasonable Force in School.' (DfEE, 1998).

The staff team members are thoroughly trained in the safest and gentlest means of holding a child which is entirely designed to enable the child to feel safe and soothed, and to bring him or her down from uncontrollable states of hyper-arousal. Whilst limits and boundaries in such circumstances can be a vital corrective emotional experience, without such an intervention (holding) the child can be left at risk of actual physical or psychological damage.

Appropriate and inappropriate touch

We are highly aware of the current atmosphere where due to fears of abuse, touch as a natural and important form of human connection has been almost vetoed in some school contexts. Our policy rests on the belief that **every** member of staff needs to appreciate the difference between appropriate and inappropriate touch. Hence all staff have to demonstrate a clear understanding of the difference. They have to show themselves to be highly aware of both the damaging and unnecessary uses of touch in an educational context. Touch is not to be used as an ill-thought out or impulsive act of futile reassurance/gratification or as a block to referral for psychological assessment.

Equally, when a child is in deep distress, the ENABLE team member is trained to know when and how sufficient connection and psychological holding have been or can be provided/ established *without* touching.

SAFE TOUCH

To ensure touch is only used appropriately the following guidelines are followed:

✓ *Parents/Carers* should be informed of the school policy around Touch.

✓ *Parents/Carers* should provide signed consent for their child to be part of the ENABLE program

✓ *Parents/Carers* wherever possible should be involved in the ENABLE Assessments and Action Plans and be regularly updated as to their child's progress through the program

✓ *Teachers and Support staff* should be trained in the ENABLE approach

✓ *Teachers and Support staff* should be trained in all aspects of safe touch

✓ *Staff members* should agree the use of safe touch in discussion with their case supervisor *and its use recorded and monitored(optional)*

✓ *2 Adult rule:* No adult should use touch when alone with a child

✓ *Use* brief, gentle contact on open clothed parts of the body: hands, arms, shoulders, head, hair, shoes.

UNSAFE TOUCH

✗ *At no point and under no circumstances* should staff members use touch to satisfy their own need for physical contact or reassurance.

✗ No unsafe touch: All staff are trained to be fully cognisant of touch that is *invasive* or which could be *confusing, traumatising or experienced as eroticising* in any way whatsoever.

✗ Should any such touch be used it would be deemed as the most serious breach of the Code of Ethics warranting the highest level of disciplinary action.

Draft May 2005

PPENDIX 2

Research evidence on the use and impact of safe touch

Safe Touch and its impact: how to enable children to know calm and contentment in later life.

Research demonstrating how early parent – child interactions which activate oxytocin have a positive influence on the brain's stress response which continue into adulthood (e.g. touch, soothing tone).
Developmental effects of oxytocin on stress response: single versus repeated exposure.
Kramer KM, Cushing BS, Carter CS. *Physiol Behav.* 2003 Sept; 79(4-5): 775–82.
The Brain–Body Center, Department of Psychiatry, University of Illinois at Chicago, Chicago IL 60612, USA. kkramer@psych.uic.edu)
'Both exogenous and endogenous oxytocin (OT) are associated with an attenuated stress response. Increased levels of OT in the early postnatal period have been shown to affect behavior and physiology ... and these effects last into adulthood, suggesting an organizational role for OT during development.'

Research demonstrating how oxytocin is capable of moderating reactivity in a key stress response system in the brain (HPA axis)
Developmental consequences of oxytocin.
Carter CS. *Physiol Behav.* 2003 Aug; 79(3): 383–97.
Development of Psychiatry, Brain-Body Center, University of Illinois at Chicago, Chicago, IL 60612, USA. scarter@psych.uic.edu)
'In adults, OT is the most abundant neuropeptide in the hypothalamus and serves integrative functions, coordinating behavioural and physiological processes. ... OT is capable of moderating behavioural responses to various stressors as well as the reactivity of the hypothalamic-pituitary-adrenal (HPA) axis.'

Research demonstrating the long-term anti-stress effect of repeated activation of oxytocin.
Uvnas-Moberg K. (Psychoneuroendocrinology. 1998 Nov; 23(8): 819–35.
Department of Physiology and Pharmacology, Karolinska Institute, Stockholm, Sweden. kerstin.uvnas-moberg@fyka.ki.se)
'Oxytocin ... also released by nonnoxious stimuli such as touch, warm temperature etc. in plasma and in cerebrospinal fluid. Consequently, oxytocin may be involved in physiological and behavioural effects induced by social interaction in a more general context ... oxytocin

exerts potent physiological antistress effects ... cortisol levels are decreased and insulin and cholecystokinin levels are increased ... After repeated oxytocin treatment weight gain may be promoted and the healing rate of wounds increased.'

... . the long-term lowering of blood pressure and of cortisol levels ... have been found to be related to an increased activity of central alpha 2-adrenoceptors. Positive social interactions have been related to health promoting effects.'

Research demonstrating how repeated activation of oxytocin is linked to long term effects of lowering blood pressure and decreasing corticosterone levels, with a resulting improved capacity to manage stress.
Oxytocin linked anti-stress effects- the relaxation and growth response.
Uvnas - Moberg K.
Acta Physiol Scand Suppl 1997 640: 38–42
Department of Physiology Swedish University of Agricultural Sciences Uppsala Sweden

'*Administration of oxytocin to male and female rats gives rise to effects of antistress nature in particular after* repeated administration." Thus a five day treatment period with oxytocin ... gives rise to ... lowering of blood pressure, ... and also a decrease of corticosterone levels and a rise of certain vagally controlled hormones. ... These effects persist several weeks after administration of oxytocin and cannot be reversed by oxytocin antagonists when established, suggesting that secondary mechanisms have been activated ... Oxytocin could be responsible for ... why relationships, social contact and networks may have health promoting effects in particular by preventing cardiovascular disease.'

Research demonstrating that high levels of touch in childhood resulted in improved responses to acute stress and lower levels of stress chemicals in later life
Maternal care, hippocampal glucocorticoid receptors, and hypothalamic-pituitary-adrenal responses to stress.
Liu D, Diorio J, Tannenbaum B, Caldji C, Francis D, Freedman A, Sharma S, Pearson D, Plotsky PM, Meaney MJ. (Science. 1997 Sept 12; 277(5332): 1659–62.
Developmental Neuroendocrinology Laboratory, Douglas Hospital Research Center, McGill University, Montreal, Canada H4H 1R3.)
'As adults, the offspring of mothers that exhibited [physical contact of infants] during the first 10 days of life showed reduced plasma adrenocorticotropic hormone and corticosterone responses to acute stress, increased hippocampal glucocorticoid receptor messenger RNA expression, enhanced glucocorticoid feedback sensitivity, and decreased levels of hypothalamic corticotropin-releasing hormone messenger RNA.'

Research demonstrating how the activation of opioids in the brain (e.g. the mother's comfort of an infant) soothes a child's distress
The biology of social attachments: opiates alleviate separation distress.
Panksepp J, Herman B, Conner R, Bishop P, Scot JP.)
Biol Psychiatry. 1978 Oct; 13(5): 607–18.
'Low doses of opiates were capable of profoundly reducing crying as well as the motor agitation they exhibit during brief periods of social isolation. Since reductions in crying could be obtained with morphine in the absence of any gross behavioural disturbances, the possibility is entertained that brain opiates may function to control the intensity of emotions arising from social separation.'

Research demonstrating that high levels of touch in childhood resulted in a far less fearful response to life in adulthood. In contrast low levels of touch in childhood resulted in increased fearfulness in later life and increased stress reactivity. Research also demonstrating that comforting maternal behaviour has a profound influence on GABA gene expression in parts of the brain, thus enabling children to be far less vulnerable to developing anxiety disorders in later life. (Early stress can actually alter the development of the GABA receptor system in the brain that mediate stress reactivity.)

Variations in Maternal Care Alter GABAA Receptor Subunit Expression in Brain Regions associated with Fear. Christian Caldji, Josie Diorio and Michael J Meaney
Developmental Neurobiology laboratory, Douglas Hospital research centre, McGill University, Montreal, Canada. (Neuropsychopharmacology, (2003) 28, 1950–1959

Under conditions of stress, the offspring of mothers who showed an increased frequency of [physical contact of their infants] exhibit more modest pituitary-adrenal responses and decreased fearfulness compared with the offspring of [low physical contact]. The increased stress reactivity of the adult offspring of [low physical contact]. mothers is associated with elevated corticotrophin-releasing factor (CRF) gene expression in both the paraventricular nucleus of the hypothalamus and the central nucleus of the amygdala.'

'Previous studies have found that the offspring of [low physical contact] mothers exhibit increased fearfulness in comparison to those [using high levels of physical contact] (Caldi et al., 1998).

In the current studies we provide evidence for a profound influence of maternal behaviour on GABBA receptor subunit gene expression that is most apparent in the basolateral and central nuclei of the amygdala, regions that are crucial for behavioural and autonomic expressions of fear (Schafe et al., 2001).'

'The effect of maternal care on GABAA receptor subunit expression may provide a mechanism for the well-established relationship between early life events and vulnerability for anxiety disorders

Studies in humans support the idea that alterations in the GABA/BZ receptor complex might form the basis of vulnerability for anxiety disorders (Gorman et al., 2000) … patients with a history of panic disorder show a significant decrease in labelling of the BZ receptor antagonist flumazenil in the orbitoprefrontal cortex and amygdala/hippocampal region in PET studies (Maliza et al., 1998). The findings are consistent with those of pharmacological measures of BZ receptor sensitivity. Subjects high on measures of neuroticism show reduced sensitivity to the BZ receptor agonist, midazolam (Glue et al., 1995) …

Patients with panic attacks or high levels of general anxiety show decreased sensitivity to BZ-induced amnesia sedation, and dampening of noradrenergic function compared with controls (Melo de Paula 1977; Oblowitz and Robins, 1983). These findings suggest that early life events might alter the development of the GABAA receptor system in brain regions that mediate stress reactivity, and thus contribute to individual differences in vulnerability to anxiety disorders (Gorman et al., 2000)'

Maternal care influence the development of stress reactivity in the offspring. These effects are accompanied by changes in corticotropin – releasing factor (CRF) expression in brain regions that regulate responses to stress. These findings are consistent with earlier reports of the effects of maternal care on GABAA/benzodizepine receptor binding and suggest that maternal care can permanently alter the subunit composition of the GABA receptor complex in brain'.

'The gamma-aminobutyric acid A (GABAA) receptor system inhibits CRF activity, particularly at the level of the amygdala and locus coeruleus (Owens et al., 1991; Skelton et al., 2000). Predictably, behavioural responses to stress are inhibited by BZ's, which exert their potent anxiolytic effect by enhancing GABA-mediated C1-currents through GABAA receptors (Barnard et al., 1998; Sieghart, 1995; McKernan and Whiting 1997; Mehta and Ticku 1999)'

Research demonstrating that touch in early childhood resulted in less fear and better mothering capacities in adulthood.
'Naturally occurring differences in maternal care are associated with the expression of oxytocin and vasopressin receptors; gender differences.'
Francis DD, Young LJ, Meaney MJ, Insel TR 2002 p 349–53
Emory University, USA

Rats receiving high levels of licking and grooming as pups are less fearful and more maternal than rats receiving low levels of maternal licking and grooming. Central pathways for oxytocin and vasopressin have been implicated in the neurobiology of anxiety and social behaviours. We assessed whether variations in maternal care associated with differences in oxytocin receptors (OTR) or vasopressin (V1a) receptors in the brain of adult offspring. In the central nucleus of the amygdala and bed nucleus of the stria terminals, OTR binding was increased in adult females, that had received high levels of maternal licking and grooming as pups.

Research demonstrating that high levels of touch in childhood positively effects the child's capacity to handle stress well in adulthood. This is due to long term changes in brain mechanisms that modulate stress reactivity.
Neurobiology of mother – infant interactions; experience and central nervous system plasticity across development and generations.
Neuroscience and Biobehavioral Reviews, May 1999, pages 673–685
A.S. Flemming, D.H. O'Day, G.W. Kraemer
Department of Psychology, University of Toronto at Mississauga, Canada
Department of Zoology, University of Toronto at Mississauga, Canada
Department of Kinesiology, Harlow Primate Laboratory, University of Wisconsin, USA

'Infant rats who received more touching and licking stimulation from the mother in the nest show a higher level of pup-licking as juveniles and as adults when presented with new-born pups … by comparison to less stimulated infants … Similar early maternal stimulation in the nest also produces a dampening of the offspring's emotional reactivity ..and stress when they become adults. Reductions in stress reactivity are attributable in part to the increased density of hippocampal glucocorticoid receptors. These receptors normally mediate negative feedback effects of circulating adrenal glucocorticoids following hypothalamic-pituitary-adrenal (HPA) activation. Stimulation-induced changes in thyroid function and brain serotonin system activity early in the postpartum period are also involved in these long-term hippocampal effects. Hence, long-term changes in brain mechanisms that modulate the stress reactivity in offspring are produced by natural variations in mothering behaviour.'

'In rhesus monkeys, measures of HPA axis activity in mothers and offspring are positively correlated. In vervet monkeys, there is substantial evidence that the style of mothering exhibited by adult daughters is similar to the style of mothering shown by their mothers. Vervet monkey mothers who engage in a high level of mother-infant ventral contact have daughters who also show high mother-infant contact. Abusive patterns of maternal care span generations as well, and the incidence of abuse varies across matrilines in pigtail macaques. … Using multivariate analysis in which these alternate influences were assessed, however, Fairbanks demonstrated that the manner in which the infants were mothered did indeed exert an effect on their mothering behaviour. Among humans, it is commonly assumed that there are often intergenerational similarities in maternal behaviour.'

Research demonstrating that touch activates oxytocin which then moderates the effect of stress chemicals.

Role of the neurohypophysis in psychological stress

Scantamburio G, Ansseau M, Legros, JJ Enephale 2001 May-June 27(3) 245–59

Service de Psychiatrie et de Psychologie Medicale CHU, Sart Tilman, Liege, Beigique.

Effects of different psychological stimuli on oxytocin (OT) and vasopression (AVP) secretion are reviewed in animals and humans. The secretion of neuropituitary hormones is also discussed in various psychiatric diseases such as anorexia nervosa, bipolar disorder, schizophrenia and obsessive – compulsive disorder. OT [has] been shown to modulate the effect of Corticotrophin-Releasing Factor (CRF) on ACTH secretion and appears to play a key role in mediating the ACTH response to stress.

… Various neuroendocrine dysregulations have been observed in psychiatric disease. Either an increase or decrease of the HPA function have been described in several illnesses … Underweight patients with anorexia nervosa have [vasopression] and reduced OT levels. These modifications could enhance the retention of cognitive distortions of aversive consequences of eating.

Research demonstrating that infants receiving high levels of physical contact were less fearful in adulthood. The touch altered the development of the neural systems in the brain that mediate fearfulness. Maternal care … regulates the development of neural systems mediating the expression of fearfulness in the rat.

Caldji, C., Tannenbaum, B., Sharma, S., Francis, D., Plotsky, P.M., & Meaney, M.J. (1998) Proceedings of the National Academy of Sciences of the United States of America, 95, 5335–5340.

[In animal research] as adults the offspring of mothers that exhibited high levels of [physical contact] showed substantially reduced behavioural fearfulness in response to novelty compared with the offspring of [low physical contact] mothers. In addition, the adult offspring of the high [physical contact] mothers showed significantly (i) increased central benzodaizepine receptor density in the central, lateral and baslateral nuclei of the amygdala as well as in the locur ceruleus. (ii) increased alpha2 adrenoreceptor density in the locus ceruleus, and (iii) descreased CRH receptor density in the locus ceruleus.

… these findings suggest that maternal care during infancy serves to 'program' behavioural responses to stress in the offspring by altering the development of the neural systems that mediate fearfulness.

Research demonstrating how evoking an image of a calming other, in their absence can activate oxytocin in the brain.

Oxytocin may mediate the benefits of positive social interaction and emotions.

Uvnas-Moberg K. (Psychoneuroendocrinology. 1998 Nov; 23(8): 819–35.

Department of Physiology and Pharmacology, Karolinska Institute, Stockholm, Sweden. kerstin.uvnas-moberg@fyka.ki.se)

'… the special properties of oxytocin, … can become conditioned to psychological state or imagery'.

Research demonstrating how social interactions which activate oxytocin in the brain can reduce stress reactivity in the brain and modulate the ANS (key bodily arousal system), perhaps accounting for health benefits of loving relationships.

Psychoneuroendocrinology. 1998 Nov; 23(8): 779–818.

Neuroendocrine perspectives on social attachment and love.

Carter CS.

Department of Biology, University of Maryland, College Park 20742, USA. cc11@umail. umd.edu)

'Positive social behaviors, including social bonds, may reduce HPA axis activity ... Central neuropeptides, and especially oxytocin and vasopressin have been implicated both in social bonding and in the central control of the HPA axis. Social interactions and attachment involve endocrine systems capable of decreasing HPA reactivity and modulating the autonomic nervous system, perhaps accounting for health benefits that are attributed to loving relationships.'

Research demonstrating that massage reduces psychological distress, and brings down blood pressure.

McNamara ME, Burnham DC, Smith C, Carroll DL. The effects of back massage before diagnostic cardiac catheterisation. Massachusetts General Hospital, Boston, USA. Altern Ther Health Med. 2003 Jan-Feb; 9(1): 50–7

A 20-minute back massage appeared to reduce systolic blood pressure, respiration, perceived psychological distress, and pain in patients awaiting a diagnostic cardiac catheterisation,

Research demonstrating that the more touch in childhood the less fearful the offspring.

Christian Caldji, Josie Diorio and Michael J Meaney, *Variations in Maternal Care Alter GABA, Receptor Subunit Expression in Brain Regions Associated with Fear.* Developmental Neuroendocrinology laboratory, Douglas Hospital Research Centre, McGill University, Montreal, Canada. Neuropsychopharmacology (2003) 28, 1950–1959, advance online publication, 23 July 2003.

Previous studies have found that the offspring of low LG-ABN mothers exhibit increased fearfulness in comparison to those of high LG-ABN dams (Caldjl et al., 1998). In the current studies, we provide evidence for a profound influence of maternal behaviour on GABA receptor subunit gene expression that is most apparent in the basolateral and central nuclei of the amygdala, regions that are crucial for behavioural and autonomic expressions of fear (Schafe et al, 2001).

Neuronal inhibition is mediated through GABA-gated CI channels, collectively know as GABA receptors. Predictably, the adult offspring of low LG-ABN mothers consistently show evidence for increased fearfulness in comparison to those of high LG-ABN mothers, (Caldji et al., 1998; Francis *et al.* 1999), and these differences are reversed with cross-fostering (Francis *et al*, 1999). Surprisingly, only a minority (30) of humans subjected to even profound trauma develop PTSD (Ressnick et al., 1993).

Research demonstrating that the activation of opioids in the amygdala has been shown to reduce stress chemicals in the brain.

Regulation of Human Affective Responses by Anterior Cingulate and Limbic and μ -Opioid Neurotransmission.

Jon-Kar Zubieta, MD, PhD; Terence A. Ketter, MD; Joshua A. Bueller, BA; Yanjan Xu, PhD; Michael R. Kilbourn, PhD; Elizabeth A. Young, MD; Robert A. Koeppe, PhD

At the level of the basolateral amygdala, μ-opioid receptor activation has been show to reduce norepinephrine release

Touch

- Carter CS. *Neuroendocrine perspectives on social attachment and love.* Department of Biology, University of Maryland, USA. Psychoneuroendocrinology. 1998 Nov; 23(8): 779–881.

Studies of pair bonding in monogamous rodents, such as prairie voles, and maternal attachment in precocial ungulates offer the most accessible animal models for the study of mechanisms underlying selective social attachments and the propensity to develop social bonds.

Positive social behaviours, including social bonds, may reduce HPA axis activity, while in some cases negative social interactions can have the opposite effect. Central neuropeptides, and especially oxytocin and vasopressin have been implicated both in social bonding and in the central control of the HPA axis. In prairie voles, which show clear evidence of pair bonds, oxytocin is capable of increasing positive social behaviours and both oxytocin and social interactions reduce activity in the HPA axis. Social interactions and attachment involve endocrine systems capable of decreasing HPA reactivity and modulating the autonomic nervous system, perhaps accounting for health benefits that are attributed to loving relationships.

GLOSSARY

The discipline of emotional and social development brings with it a diverse language, and a range of concepts meaning similar, connected but slightly different things. These definitions are often used differently and interchangeably by different people – we offer the definitions below to ensure you understand how the terminology is used here.

Emotional and social development is the process of developing awareness, understanding and choices about behaviours in intra-personal and interpersonal relationships and social situations. This learning is facilitated in, through and about relationships. It is developmental in that tasks are addressed and learning is acquired in a sequential way throughout life. As the person matures, so their understanding, attitudes and skills increase as long as appropriate learning opportunities and support are available. Over time, and through experiencing different qualities of relationship, the child or young person acquires knowledge and understanding, develops attitudes and explores values, and tries out new ways of doing things to extend and develop skills. Emotional development is an ongoing process influenced by the quality of the earliest relationships with primary carers, which continues through the early years into puberty, adolescence and adulthood. It informs, shapes and gives meaning to social relationships. At best this supports the young person to create and sustain meaningful, creative contact with others so that s/he moves from dependence to independence and then interdependence.

Emotional health and well-being describes both a state of being and a capacity to thrive with the right nurturing, care, education and opportunities. This will be 'good enough' to cope well with everyday living including setbacks and difficult circumstances.

Mental health is not just the absence of mental disorder. The positive dimension of mental health is stressed in the World Health Organization's definition of health as contained in its constitution; 'Health is a state of complete physical, mental and social well-being and not merely the absence of disease or infirmity'. Mental health is often used inaccurately to describe mental illness.

Emotional health and well-being and mental illness have traditionally been seen on a single continuum, with emotional health and well-being on one end of the continuum and mental illness on the other. However, the National Healthy School Standard Guidance on emotional health and well-being (Health Development Agency, 2004) argues that this is too narrow a perspective. A person with a mental illness may have a positive sense of emotional health and well-being, and this can help in the management of mental health problems. It also states that the positive promotion of emotional health and well-being can help in the prevention of mental health problems.

Emotional intelligence is the cognitive capacity that informs our understanding of our selves (intra-personally) and ourselves in relation to others (interpersonally). It supports us to be able to think about our feelings, recognise them and know the sensations that accompany them. Being 'emotionally intelligent' requires having the awareness and skills to be able to take responsibility for our feelings and our behaviours.

Emotional capacity includes emotional resilience, emotional resourcefulness and emotional reflexivity. The degree of its presence or absence determines how well we are able to be open, creative and available to learn, develop and thrive.

Emotional resilience is the ability to be flexible and creative in the face of life's challenges and difficulties. It includes being able to deal with uncertainty, opposition, disappointment and failure in non-defensive ways, as well as being able to learn from times of contradiction and paradox. It helps us to bounce back emotionally under adverse or difficult conditions and to persevere when the going gets tough.

Emotional resourcefulness is the set of attitudes, values and skills that support us to ask for and use help; to identify resources and be able to organise and use them and to be able to support ourselves and others to make appropriate and effective choices.

Emotional reflexivity is the capacity to be able to reflect on one's feelings and experiences rather than just react to them. It includes being able to think about and reflect on social situations and relationship difficulties in order to gain understanding, extend choices and solve problems.

Self-esteem is how we feel about ourselves and how in control of our lives we feel. It includes a sense of worth or value, a sense of identity, a degree of self-agency (being able to go for what we want and need) and a degree of self-advocacy (being able to promote ourselves, stand up for what we believe in and ask for what we need). It is not a constant and at times people feel bad and other times feel good about themselves, but having good enough self-esteem is evidenced by a core ongoing sense of being 'good enough' as we are.

FURTHER READING

Batmanghelidjh, C. (2006) *Shattered Lives: Children Who Live with Courage and Dignity*. London: Jessica Kingsley.

Blake, S. (2006) *A Whole School Approach to Personal, Social, Health Education and Citizenship*. 2nd edn. London: National Children's Bureau.

Blake, S. and Frances, G. (2004) *Promoting Children and Young People's Participation through the National Healthy School Standard*. London: Health Development Agency.

Blake, S. and Plant, S. (2005) *Addressing Inequalities and Inclusion through Personal, Social, Health Education and Citizenship*. London: National Children's Bureau.

FTC Projects Ltd and The Modbury Group (2002) *ENABLE (Emotional Needs, Achieving, Behaving and Learning in Education)*.

Health Development Agency (2002) *National Healthy School Standard: Staff Health and Well Being*. London: Health Development Agency.

Health Development Agency (2003) *Promoting Emotional Health and Well Being through the National Healthy School Standard*. London: Health Development Agency.

Job, N. and Frances, G. (2004) *Childhood Bereavement: Developing the Curriculum and Pastoral Support*. London. National Children's Bureau.

Morris, E. and Casey, J. (2006) *Developing Emotionally Literate Staff*. London: Paul Chapman Publishing

National Children's Bureau (NCB) (2005) *Cards for Life: Promoting Emotional and Social Development*. London: National Children's Bureau.

National Children's Bureau (NCB) (2006) *Getting It Together: A Resource Pack for Working with Young People on Emotional Health and Well-being*. London: National Children's Bureau.

Parsons, M. and Blake, S. (2004) *Peer Support: An Overview.* London: National Children's Bureau and Peer Support Forum.

Sense Interactive CD-ROM (2006) *Making Sense of Growing Up and Staying Safe*. Kent: Sense Interactive CDS.

Authors' Note:

National Children's Bureau *Spotlight* series provides practitioners in education, health, care, youth and community settings with the information and guidance they need to improve the lives of the children and young people they work with. www.ncb.org.uk Tel: 020 7843 1901

A Voice for the Child in Care (VCC) www.vcc-uk.org

A national charity committed to empowering children and young people in public care and to campaign for change to improve their lives. Tel: 020 7833 5792

Anti-Bullying Alliance (ABA) www.anti-bullyingalliance.org.uk

The Alliance was founded by NSPCC and the National Children's Bureau in 2002. It is hosted and supported by the NCB. The Alliance brings together 65 organisations into one network with the aim of reducing bullying and creating safer environments in which children and young people can live, grow, plan and learn. Tel: 020 7843 1901

Antidote (Campaign for Emotional Literacy) www.antidote.org.uk

Promotes the development of emotional literacy through consultancy, conferences, publications and training. Tel: 020 7247 3355

Brain Gym – Educational Kinesiology www.braingym.org

A worldwide network dedicated to enhancing living and learning through the science of movement. For more than 30 years and in over 80 countries, they have been helping children, adults, and seniors to learn *anything* faster and more easily, perform better at sports, be more focused and organised, start and finish projects with ease, overcome learning challenges and reach new levels of excellence

Childhood Bereavement Network www.childhoodbereavementnetwork.org.uk

The Network 'seeks to ensure that all children and young people in the UK, together with their families and other care-givers, including professional carers, can easily access a choice of high-quality local and national information, guidance and support to enable them to manage the impact of death on their lives'. Tel: 020 7843 6309 or email cbn@ncb.org.uk

ENABLE (Emotional Needs Achieving Behaving and Learning in Education) training and consultancy www.enable-online.com

Provides training and consultancy on emotional development, social, emotional and behavioural difficulties and improving behaviour in educational settings. Tel: 01548 843992

Institute for Arts in Therapy and Education/Centre for Child Mental Health www.arts psychotherapy.org

Runs conferences, courses (from certificate to Master's level) on all aspects of working with children on matters of emotional development and mental health, including a Certificate in Emotional

Literacy for Children training for all adults who work with children. Tel: 020 7704 2534 or email info@artspsychotherapy.org

Massage in Schools Association www.massageinschoolsassociation.org.uk and www. massageinschools.com

The Massage in Schools Association supports Instructors trained with the Massage in Schools Programme (MISP), a peer massage programme for children of primary school age. They provide support and training for schools. Tel: 07773 044 282

Mental Health Foundation www.mentalhealth.org.uk

A national charity working in mental health and learning disabilities. Provides information, publications and resources on mental health issues including problems, treatments and strategies for living with mental distress. Tel: 020 7802 0300

National Children's Bureau www.ncb.org.uk

The NCB provides training and resources on all aspects of emotional and social development and emotional health and well-being. Tel: 020 7843 6000 or email training@ncb.org.uk ncb@centralbooks.com

Qualifications and Curriculum Authority (QCA) www.qca.org.uk

The QCA is committed to building a world-class education and training framework. It regulates, develops and modernises the curriculum, assessments, examinations and qualifications. Tel: 020 7509 5555

Royal College of Psychiatrists www.repsych.ac.uk

Publishes a series of leaflets for the general public on common mental health issues, called Help is at Hand. Tel: 020 7235 2351

School of Emotional Literacy www.schoolofemotional-literacy.com

Trains professionals in the use of emotional literacy in their work; runs a certified course in emotional literacy for anyone involved in supporting children. Tel: 01452 741106

Schools Health Education Unit www.sheu.org.uk

The SHEU provides survey, research and publishing services. We work with a wide range of people involved in the planning, providing and commissioning of health and education in the UK and overseas. Tel: 01392 667272

Sowelu Associates www.soweluassociates.co.uk

Offers training and consultancy on all aspects of emotional health and well-being and the development of emotionally competent organisations. Tel: 01548 843992

The National Emotional Literacy Interest Group (NELIG) www.nelig.com

Promotes emotional literacy for adults and children.

The PSHE Subject Association www.pshe-association.org.uk

The association provides a central support network for teachers of PSHE, giving them a focal point to receive advice, gather and share examples of good practice and promote existing guidance. Tel: 020 7843 1916 or email info@pshe-association.org.uk

The Sainsbury Centre for Mental Health www.scmh.org.uk

Works to improve the quality of life for people with mental health problems. Carries out research, policy work and analysis to improve practice and influence policy in public services. Work focuses on those areas where the centre can make the greatest difference to people's lives. Its priorities are mental health care in the criminal justice system and the employment of people with mental health problems. Tel: 020 7827 8300

The Who Cares? Trust www.rhrn.thewhocarestrust.org.uk

A national charity working to improve public care for children and young people who are separated from their families and living in residential or foster care. Promotes the interests of children and young people in public care and works with all those interested in their well-being. Produces resources for children and young people. Tel: 020 7251 3117

Trust for the Study of Adolescence www.tsa.uk.com

Seeks to improve knowledge and understanding about adolescence and young adulthood, main areas of work are communication, emotional well-being, health, parenting and family life, social action and youth justice. Provides resources and training and undertakes research. Tel: 01273 693311

Wired for Health www.wiredforhealth.gov.uk

A series of websites providing health information for a range of audiences that relates to the National Curriculum and Healthy Schools. There is information for teachers, Healthy School co-ordinators and education professionals; and a series of interactive websites, for children and young people aged 5 to 16 years, covering a range of health issues.

Young Minds www.youngminds.org.uk

This is a national charity committed to improving the mental health of all children and young people. Its website has sections for professionals, young people and parents. It also produces a range of leaflets, which can be downloaded or ordered. Tel: 020 7336 8445

REFERENCES

Ahmad et al. (2003) *Listening to children and young people*. University of the West of England.

Axline, V. (1996) *Dibs: In Search of Self*. London: Penguin.

Ball, S. (2006) Bystanders and Bullying. A Summary of Research for Anti-Bullying Week 2006. London: NCB on behalf of the Anti-Bullying Alliance.

Batmanghelidjh, C. (2006) *Shattered Lives: Children who Live with Courage and Dignity*. London: Jessica Kingsley.

Berne, E. (1973) *Sex in Human Loving*. London: Penguin.

Bird, J. (2006) *'The beautiful dance of relationship – emotional health, well-being and learning'*, paper presented at Blackpool Local Authority PSHE Conference, Blackpool Hilton, 30 June.

Bird, J. and Gerlach, L. (2005) *Promoting Emotional Health and Well Being in Secure Units*. London: NCB.

Bird, J. and Gerlach, L. (2005a) *Promoting Emotional Health and Well Being in Secure Units*. London: National Children's Bureau.

Bird, J. and Gerlach, L. (2005b) *Improving the Emotional Health and Well-being of Young People in Secure Care: Training for Staff in Local Authority Secure Children's Homes*. London: National Children's Bureau.

Blake, S. (2003) *Young Gay Men Talking: Key Issues and Ideas for Action*. London: Working With Men.

Blake, S. (2005) 'Editorial: Health education and young people: it's time to join up!', *Health Education'*, 105 (4): pp. 245–48.

Blake, S. and Crow, F. (eds) (2005) *Journeys: Children and Young People Talk about Bullying*. London: Office of the Children's Commissioner.

Blake, S. and Navidi, U. (2005) *Dangerous Highs: Calls to Childline about Volatile Substance Abuse. London: National Children's Bureau with Childline*.

Bowlby, J. (1969) *Attachment and Loss*. Vol. I. London: Hogarth Press.

Britton, F. (1998) *The Heart of a Teacher: Identity and Integrity in Teaching*. (unpublished).

Cairns, E. and Lloyd, K. (2005) *Stress at Sixteen: Research update*. Belfast: ARK Northern Ireland Social and Political Archive.

Claxton, G. (1999) *Wise-up – The Challenge of Lifelong Learning*. London: Bloomsbury.

Cohen, E. (1994) *Designing Group Work: Strategies for the Heterogenous Classroom*. New York: Teachers College Press.

Cooper, V. (2005) *Support Staff in Schools: promoting the emotional and social development of children in schools*. London: NCB.

Corlyon, J. and McGuire, C. (1999) *Teenage Pregnancy and Parenthood: The views and experiences of young people in public care*. London: National Children's Bureau. www.antibullyingalliance.org

De Silva, S. and Blake, S. (2006) *Positive Guidance on Aspects of Personal, Social and Health Education*. London: National Children's Bureau.

Department for Culture, Media and Sport (DCMS) (2004) *Getting Serious about play – a review of children's play*, p 6. London: DCMS.

Department for Education and Employment (DfEE) (1998) *New guidance on the use of Reasonable Force in Schools*. Circular number 10/98. London: DfEE.

Department for Education and Skills (DfES) (2002) *Minority Ethnic Pupils in Mainly White Schools*. Research Report 365. London: DfES.

Department for Education and Skills (DfES) (2005) *The ACIS KnowHow Pack*. London: DfES.

Department of Health (DH) (2004) *Choosing Health: Making Healthy Choices Easier*. London: Department of Health.

Department of Health (DH) (2004) *National Service Framework for Children, Young People and Maternity Services: The Mental Health and Psychological Well Being of Children*. London: Department of Health.

Easton, E. and Carpentieri J.D. (2004) *Can I Talk to You Again? Restoring the emotional and mental well being of children and young people*. London: Childline.

Every Child Matters. London: HMSO.

Gerlach, L. and Bird, J. (1999) 'What's love got to do with it? Sex education and emotional literacy', *Sex Education Matters*, 10–11.

Goleman, D. (1996) *Emotional Intelligence: Why It Can Matter More than IQ*. London: Bloomsbury.

Green, H., Mcginnity, A., Meltzer, H., Ford, T. and Goodman, R. (2005) *Mental Health of Children and Young People in Great Britain, 2004*. Harlow: Palgrave Macmillan.

Hartley-Brewer, E. (2002) *Stepping Forward: Working Together through Peer Support*. London: National Children's Bureau.

Hawton, K., Rodham, K. and Evans, E. (2006) *By their Own Young Hand: Deliberate Self-harm and Suicidal Ideas in Adolescents*. London: Jessica Kingsley.

HeadsUpScotland (2005) *The Voice of Children and Young People about Mental Health*. Glasgow: HeadsUpScotland.

Health Development Agency (2002) National Healthy School Standard: Staff Health and well Being. London: Health Development Agency.

Health Development Agency (2004) *Promoting Emotional Health and Well-being through the National Healthy School Standard*. London: Health Development Agency.

Horton, C. (ed.) (2005) *Working with Children 2006–7*. London: Society Guardian and Sage.

Hughes, D.A. (2002) Course handout: 'Attachment and deeply troubled young people'.

Illesley-Clarke, J. and Dawson, C. (1989) *Growing Up Again: Preventing Ourselves, Parenting our Children*. San Francisco, CA: Harper and Row.

Lucas, P. and Liabo, K. (2004) *Breakfast Clubs and School Fruit Schemes*. London: National Children's Bureau.

Mason, A. and Palmer, A. (1996) *Queer Bashing: A National Survey of Hate Crimes against Lesbians and Gay Men*. London: Stonewall.

Matthews, B. (2003) *Improving emotional development through science*. London: Calouste Gulbenkian Foundation.

McConville, B. (1998) *The State They're In – Young People in Britain Today*. Leicester: Youth Work Press.

McConville, B. (2003) *I'm in Control: Calls to Childline about Eating Disorders*. London: Childline.

Mcgrellis, S., Henderson, S., Holland, J., Sharpe, S. and Thomson, R. (2000) *Through the Moral Maze: a quantitative study of young people's values*. London: Tuffnell Press.

McLaughlin, C. with Alexander, E. (2004) *Reframing Personal, Social and Emotional Education: Relationships, Inclusion, Diversity, Agency, Participation and Dialogue*. Warwick: NAPCE.

McVeigh, J., Hughes, K., Bellis, M.A., Reed, E., Ashton, J.R. and Syed, Q. (2005) *Violent Britain: People, Prevention and Public Health*. Liverpool: Liverpool John Moores University.

Mencap (2000) *Living in Fear: The Need to Combat Bullying of People with Learning Difficulties*. London: Mencap.

Mental Health Foundation (1999) *Bright Futures: Promoting Children and Young People's Mental Health*. London: Mental Health Foundation.

Morris, E. and Casey, J. (2006) *Developing Emotionally Literate Staff*. London: Paul Chapman Publishing.

National Children's Bureau (NCB) (2005) *Cards for life. Promoting Emotional and Social Development*. London: National Children's Bureau.

National Children's Bureau (NCB) with Drug Education Forum (DEF) (2004) *Be Aware: Young People, Alcohol and Other Drugs*. London: National Children's Bureau.

National Children's Bureau (NCB) (2006) *Getting It Together: a Resource Pack for Working with Young People on Emotional Health and Well-being*. London: National children's Bureau.

National Health and Lifestyles Surveys in Ireland (2002) www.ark.ac.uk/nilt/2002 www.ark.ac.uk/nilt/2002

NHSS (2004) *Achieving Healthy School Status*. London: Department for Education and Skills and Department of Health.

Office for Standards in Education (Ofsted) (2005) *Managing Challenging Behaviour*. HMI 2363. London: Ofsted.

Office for Standards in Education (Ofsted) (2006) *Extended Services in Schools and Children's Centres*. HMI 2609. London: Ofsted.

O'Reilly, D. and Stevenson, M. (2003) 'Mental health in Northern Ireland: Have "the Troubles" made it worse?', *Journal of Epidemiological Community Health*, 57: 488–92.

Parsons, M. and Blake, S. (2004) *Peer Support: An Ovrerview*. London: National Children's Bureau and Peer Support forum.

Qualifications and Curriculum Authority (2000) *All our Futures: creativity in the classroom*. London: QCA.

Schools Health Education Unit (SHEU) (2004) *Trends: Young People and Emotional Health and Well-being*. Exeter: Schools Health Education Unit.

Stacey, H. (1996) 'Mediation into schools does go', *Journal for Pastoral and Personal and Social Education*, 14 (2): 7–10.

Stanford, G. (1990) *Developing Effective Classroom Groups:* London: Acora Books.

Stern, *The Interpersonal World of an Infant*. New York: Basic Books.

Stockdale, D. and Katz, A. (2002) *Wassup? The Report of a Project Exploring More than One Thousand Young People's Views on Health and Well Being in Waltham Forest and Redbridge, London 2002*. East Molesey: Young Voice.

Sutherland, M. (2005) *2005 Literature Review and Research Survey on the Role of Touch in Emotional, Social and Brain Development*. London: IATE/CCMH.

Teenage Pregnancy Independent Advisory Group (TPIAS) and the Sexual Health Independent Advisory Group (SMIAS) (2005) *Time for Action: Personal, Social and Health Education in Schools*. London: HMSO.

United Nations (1989) (ratified in the UK 1991) *The Convention on the Rights of the Child*. Adopted by the General Assembly of the United Nations on 20 November 1989. Geneva: Defence for the Children International and the United Nations Children's Fund.

United Nations Children's Fund (UNICEF) (2005) 'Behind closed doors: the impact of domestic violence on children' London: UNICEF.

Weare, K. (2004) 'Work on the structure and function of the brain is revolutionizing our understanding of the role of emotion in education', *Health Education*, 104 (1): 5–7.

Williams, K., Chambers, M., Loyan, S. and Robinson, D. (1996) 'Association of common health symptoms with bullying in primary school children', *British Medical Journal*, 313: 17–19.

World Health Organization (2001) *Mental Health: Strengthening Mental Health Promotion*. Factsheet 220 www.who.int.

Worthy, A. (2005) *Supporting Children and Young People through Transition*. London: National Children's Bureau.

Wren, A. (2006) 'The pressure to look good', *Young People Now*, 25–31 January, pp. 14–15.

INDEX

Added to a page number 'f' denotes a figure and 't' denotes notes.